KISSED BY A MINNOW,

PINCHED BY A CRAB

A visually unique perspective on the human nature of the Chesapeake Bay

MD II AH

JAMES PARKER

Dedicated to:
Jean Adams Parker
grandmother of Dan and Taylor

Published by James Parker Photography Group
P/O Box 1353 Severna Park, Maryland 21146

Library of Congress Catalog Number: 00-091860

"The peculiar power of photography lies in its ability to compel belief in the truthfulness of what is represented."

Andy Grundberg

CONTENTS

Introduction .... pg. 10

James Parker

"The Wisdom of
Miss Nettie's Fritters" .... pg. 18

Hellen Chapple

Moral Culpability .... pg. 24

"Early years of watermen
were a different world"

Keepers of the Bay .... pg. 27

Steve Burch

Agents of Consequence .... pg. 41

"Lawmakers must realize overregulating
the Bay can corrode communities"

Chesapeake Bay Facts and a Note
About Kent Island Piracy .... pg. 54
Some of which are even true

"The Straight Facts
About Providing Seafood
for the World's Table" .... pg. 56
National Fisheries Institute

Dispatches from the Mythical
Town of Oysterback .... pg. 72
Hellen Chapple

Girly Job .... pg. 78
Steve Burch

Facts About the Chesapeake
Bay Watershed .... pg. 76
USDA & Fish and Wildlife

Island of High Achievers .... pg. 102
"Smith Island crab pickers legalized
with founding of co-op"

Patience and a Little Help
from Mother Nature .... pg. 106

"Waterman's wife grows to appreciate new lifestyle"

Beauty is Where You Look .... pg. 107

"Oysterman awed by the natural beauty of his catch"

Fish are Like Birds .... pg. 111

"Week long closure of gill net fishery
prompted by plethora of fish"

Epilogue .... pg. 112

Appendix A .... pg. 113

Note to collectors of black and white photography

Appendix B .... pg. 114

List of photographic plates

Appendix C .... pg. 120

Brief descriptions of commercial seafood
and harvesting styles

Appendix D .... pg. 126

Selected references

The Morality of Saving the Bay ...... pg. 128

"Everything comes from nature, including the things
that do not appear to resemble it."

Rodger Bordier

LEARNING THE LORE OF THE BAY

Most of the information before you was presented in one form or another inside the Chautaugua tent at Chesapeake Appreciation Days. My thanks go to Betty Duty for her support and management, along with Lois L. Goldstein, Jeff Holland, Larry Chowning, Hon Lawson, Ralph Eshelman, Wade Murphy, Rodger Ethier, Jack Sherwood, Donald Shomette, Alice Bulter Bradshaw and Janis Marshall for sharing their lives. Bill Sieling originally proposed the Chautaugua idea, Martha Turnage dotted the i's and crossed the t's, and Sue Beinger was the great factotum.

Chesapeake Appreciation Days was a wonderful celebration of the Chesapeake Bay. Too bad it rained three years in a row.

"We may all be to blame. Precipitation figures from 1979 to 1995 recorded off North America's Atlantic coast shows that 22 percent more rain falls on Saturdays than on Mondays. Monday's figures are the week's lowest, and then the amount increases daily through the workweek, says Randy Cervenny, an Arizona State University geographer. He suspects that a pollution buildup caused by weekday driving helps bring weekend rain."

National Geographic Vol. 195, No. 3

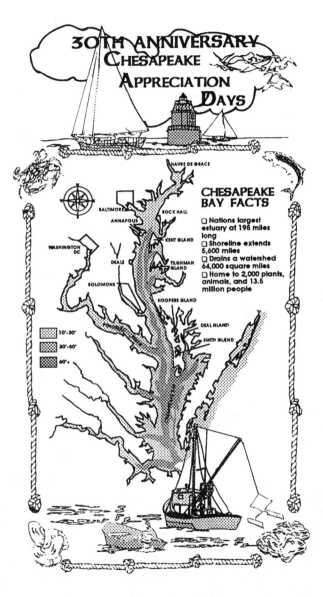

30TH ANNIVERSARY CHESAPEAKE APPRECIATION DAYS

CHESAPEAKE BAY FACTS

☐ Nations largest estuary at 195 miles long
☐ Shoreline extends 8,600 miles
☐ Drains a watershed 64,000 square miles
☐ Home to 2,000 plants, animals, and 13.6 million people

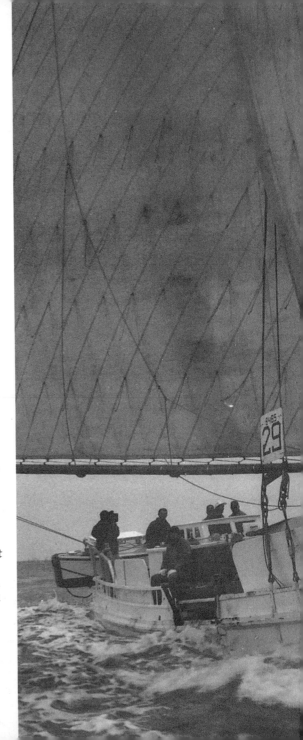

INTRODUCTION

I am bewitched with the swish of water. I am fascinated by its inter-dependent life and the fleeting appreciation of life taken.

Had I been born a poet rather than having been trained as a photographer, I would be writing with wit and wisdom of the true nature of my Chesapeake Bay. Instead, I can only offer flat, two-dimensional images of 1/60th of a second of real life, other people's words, and the view of a five year-old student sociologist from the red planet Mars.

The scope of the photography is limited to images taken for the Maryland Waterman's Gazette between 1982 and 1998, and driven by my lust to understand the environment of my youth, which began as an infant in the cool shade beneath a community pier where the minnows would nibble at my toes. I now understand, some 42 years later, that the primary nature of the Chesapeake Bay is to provide food, and minnows are the reason why this high-dollar

REBECCA T. RUARK: Oyster Dredge Boat License #29; she is part of the last fleet of boats working under sail in the United States, commonly known as Skipjacks, which refers to the style of the sails and not to the type of boat or hull design. These boats are an icon of the Chesapeake Bay complete with resentment and endearment. Competition between captains created many myths and much of the lore that surrounds the Skipjacks.

ANNE ARUNDEL COUNTY
Broadneck

architectural photographer spent 16 years taking pictures on traditional boats for no money, exposing film to light in search of an answer to a question I have never been able to formulate.

There is no specific time-line to the photography, and the only structure in this book is geographic. All else is fluid, rhythm, and layers that are scientifically unimportant.

If there is a beginning, a middle, or an end, it is only in the context of the photographic moment, the moment when the shutter is released and light is inverted and transformed by glass to be recorded on celluloid film. What becomes of the wave lengths of

light is an impression of energy, a reflection of the interplay of surface and light in search of expression.

To understand my parallel between photography, minnows, and Watermen, it is necessary to recognize the Chesapeake Bay as a large-hipped female who is top-heavy, left-handed, and finely sloped. She is a breeder blessed with grace and a great passionate energy. Her horizontal movements are the consequences of gravitational attraction, and the layers of salt and fresh water are the countenance of centrifugal force. Her prolific abilities are simply that the bottom of the bay is very close to the top, and light penetrates. She is unique: both complex and simple, lovingly moody, exciting, virile, and flirtatious.

But she is stressed by the demands of the twentieth century. Unfortunately, for many people, the perceived 'bogeyman' is the one who knows her most intimately, the commercial fisherman. He is the 'top' carnivore and the largest visual predator, an easy target for finger pointing. We think what we see is debauchery and it irritates us. Yet the Waterman understands her like no other. His grip on the nuances of water, wind, tide, salinity, and temperature, in

"All Maryland citizens have much to gain directly and indirectly in and through the preservation and recognition of Bay history and culture."

Governor J. Millard Tawes 1965

practical application, is unique and unmatched.

There is a touch of insolence about his relationship with our heroine, but those I have recorded on film and tape are respectful family men and women who enjoy an honest day's work and are among themselves great storytellers. Much of the romance and most of the myths about working on the water come from the "good" stories of the lawless daring-do of a few men. It is their independence that we label "outlaw". Yet there is much that we can learn from their individual work ethic and the knowledge of the bay hidden within their stories.

The Watermen have had a long and honorable tradition of oral learning. There are no college classes titled "Outsmarting Fish." There are no signs that say, "stop here and catch a crab," just generations of story-telling and observation, which are the common bonds of all fishermen.

In the years before television, oral communication was the entertainment that provided education. It is still the method by which Watermen learn their trade. Adaptability, patience, and awareness are the principal qualities of the successful Waterman.

My generation, the one of television, never knew an environment that was to be feared and conquered. We watched our parents put men on the moon and took for granted electricity, pasteurization, and refrigeration. Easy travel was a gift that helped create a sense of unearned credit in "taming" nature. And our world consisted of unlimited natural resources, which we now know are not infinite. Mega agricultural business or family farm, playground or breeding ground, how do I teach my children about impact and effect, balance of resource and need? Not only their need, but the need of others as well? What is the true nature of the Chesapeake Bay, and in what form does she wish to be saved?

Environmentalists, recreational users, and the commercial fishing industry are seemingly locked in contest with the state for control of the Bay. Each has a driving agenda. Each has an urgent priority. Each has something important to offer the community.

In the outcome of this battle lies the fate of our larger community. We have isolated ourselves with our 45-minute commute to work in a concrete cubicle and have lost our ability to connect. We have forgotten what it is like to be kissed by a minnow.

There is a spirituality and a knowing that comes from harvesting the Chesapeake Bay that should not be overlooked. The Waterman community is an important part of the equation of preservation and through them we can better understand the Chesapeake Bay.

James Parker

"If you lose the commercial fisheries, you lose a huge constituency for saving the Bay."

Will Baker, President
Chesapeake Bay Foundation

FREEWHEELING WATERMAN. "Within the last 165 years, Maryland lawmakers have devoted more legislation to matters pertaining to the Chesapeake Bay than to any other single priority. The law tells our hero where he can fish, when he can fish, how much he can fish, and how big what he catches must be. Beyond that, he is told in no uncertain terms how his boat must be appointed with so many life preservers, fire extinguishers, lights, horns, bells, and the like."

George C. Carey

The Wisdom of Miss Nettie's Fritters

Fiction by Hellen Chapple

On the kitchen wall, the cat clock ticks away the twilight hours. The rhinestone eyes slide one way, the black plastic tail the other. Miss Nettie Leery stubs out her Salem in the big glass ashtray on the table. When her visitor is not looking, she glances first up at the cat clock, then out the window, where snow is falling in small mean flakes. Deep inside the still, darkened parlor, the wind moans and whines in the chinks beneath the doors, feeling at the window sashes, looking for entry. But the kitchen is warm and steamy.

"Listen to that. She's up and down the mast tonight," Miss Nettie says, rising from the table and brushing cigarette ash from her massive bosom. "Don't think your folks will come lookin' for you on a night like this, no matter what you did. Anyway, they canceled the Rutger Hauer Film Festival up at the Community Center. So, as long as you're here, why don't you stay and see how I make my oyster fritters? It's a family secret, passed from my grandmother to me, and from me to you."

Miss Nettie opens the refrigerator, taking things out and setting them on the counter. "They're not gourmet or fancy, just plain Oysterback cooking," she tells her visitor, grunting as she bends to retrieve the big iron skillet from the place where it lives in the oven. "Fetch me over that big ironstone bowl, that's a lamb," she says, dolloping out two walnut sized spoonfuls of Crisco into the pan. "Now, you set that on low heat while you build your batter.

"That young doctor would have a fit if he could see me makin' oyster fritters. When I was your age, we fried them in lard. Four times a year, Dad would go up to Baltimore on the skipjack and come back with a barrel of flour, a sack of sugar, and a fifty-pound can of lard. He didn't know nothing about cholesterol, and he lived to be ninety-seven!

"No one on our side of the family's ever had a heart attack. Cholesterol! Ugh!" She breaks an egg on the side of the bowl, whisking it with a fork. Opening a pint mason jar of shucked oysters, she spoons them into the bowl and stirs them carefully.

"I was just your age when my Me-Mom showed me how to make oyster fritters. That gold and red set of china was her wedding set. It came all the way from China on a clipper ship. Keep an eye on that skillet, don't let it heat up too fast. No, I daresay that your mom and your daddy won't come lookin' for you on a night like this, no matter what you broke," she assures her visitor.

She opens the red and white rooster canister on the counter and dumps about a quarter cup of flour into the bowl with the oysters. Then she adds salt and pepper. "Get out in the pantry and fetch me the baking powder. Not the baking soda, the baking powder. Now watch, you add a teaspoon to the batter, then three tablespoons Half and Half.

"When I was your age, I knocked over my mother's Chelsea Bow cat, smashed it into a thousand pieces. Oh she was fit to be tied! I went to **my** Me-Mom and hid there. Now, watch me. I fold it all together, don't stir it up with this here wooden spoon. You stir, you break the oysters apart. Is that Crisco smokin' in the skillet now? Fine."

"What did it really look like before television, fast cars and jet airplanes? As soon as we began to travel faster in this country, the importance of place got lost."

Vine Deloria

Carefully, Miss Nettie ladles the batter into the skillet. "Now, some of the ladies at church, they make fritters the size of a pancake. Use pancake mix, too. Don't let me catch you doin' that! You want your fritters to be the size of the mouth of a drinking glass, no bigger." As the batter hits the hot pan, it sizzles, sending a delicious aroma into the moist and steamy kitchen.

"Now, when the edges of the fritters are crisp and brown, and the batter's bubbling on the inside, it's time to turn it. You run and get a jar of those green beans I canned last August and put that in the microwave. And get the silver out and set the table. We'll use the gold and red china tonight, for special. And we'll have some watermelon pickle and a taste of that chow-chow you like, OK?"

The fritters slowly turn from buff to a crisp golden brown, and Miss Nettie flips them over with the spatula. "Now," she says, "run and get me a grocery sack from the shelf. A paper one, not one of those nasty plastic ones. That's what we drain the fritters on. From somewhere, the cat appears, attracted by the smell of food. It rubs against Miss Nettie's legs. "Beggar," she says, but she slips it a small oyster anyway. The cat seizes it and disappears.

As Miss Nettie eases the fritters from the skillet onto the coarse brown paper bag, the wind picks up, howling and rattling at the kitchen windows. "That's the devil trying to escape the weather," Miss Nettie says complacently.

The fritters, round and crispy, stain the coarse paper dark brown. Miss Nettie ladles out more batter into the skillet. "Never stop when the pan's hot," she says.

Beneath the whining of the blizzard, she hears a sound as she cocks her head to one side, listening. A faint smile plays on her lips.

"Best set another place," she commands. "We're going to have some company. Yes, I imagine it is your Daddy, but I doubt that he'll be angry with you by now. Don't you think that he's had time to realize that you're more important to him than a fishing reel? By the time he's realized you're gone, and he's driven all over the place looking for you, he'll be more scared than angry. And hungry, too. Oyster fritters are a great pacifier for anyone."

Miss Nettie watches, unsurprised, as the headlights of a truck move slowly up her lane. "How did I know it was him? Why child I'd know the sound of that truck anywhere! Heard it all the way down at the corner of Black Dog Road. You go put the porch light on for him, and tell your Daddy not to come any further than the mud room in his boots. I don't want my clean floors tracked up with mud. Run, now, don't let him stumble around in that snow!"

When she is alone in the kitchen, she helps herself to a small, beautifully round fritter. The cake is crumbly and light; the warm oysters break apart in her mouth, delicate and salty. Miss Nettie closes her eyes. "Perfect," she sighs. "Just perfect."

Helen Chapple

WIND FOR POWER. "The Chesapeake Bay's weather comes either in small aggravating bits and pieces — daily fogs, thunderstorms, feather-white sou'westers, winter freeze-ins — or else it comes in a devastating dollop such as Hurricane Agnes, which blew through in the early summer of 1972. Agnes dumped such a load of fresh water into the bay and its tributaries that the saline quality of the waters changed markedly and so did the reproductive cycle of bay life.

For whatever reasons, the bay seems to be able to sustain overwrought nature better than it can man's pollutants. According to the watermen, it is not storms like Agnes or even their own overharvesting that has brought about the depletion in fish and oyster catches, but the runoff of nitrogen-rich fertilizer from shoreside farms and the effluence of sewage treatment plants. This pollution has drowned tight the oxygen supply, choked off the once-abundant oysters and finfish.

Some like Russell Dize of Tilghman Island lay the blame at the state's doorstep. "If they'd been controlling the sewage plants and industries like they're supposed to, we wouldn't have any shortage," he told a reporter from the Washington Post in the fall of 1984. H. C. Elliott of Brooms Island claims that the chemical runoff in Patuxent killed off all the grasses that used to protect the shedding crabs and give the ducks something to feed on."

George G. Carey

"The men who work the Chesapeake Bay are echoes of that day when most Americans made their living close to nature."

James A. Michener

MORAL CULPABILITY
"Early years of Watermen were a different world"
Letter to the Editor of the Waterman's Gazette

I was born and raised on the Magothy River during the 30's and 40's. Dad was a Waterman and a farmer. The land and the water fed and supported our family. The river was quite different during my growing up years. Whenever you saw a boat on the river after the summer season, you would know the captain at the wheel by name.

Summer was the time to take a dip after a day in the fields. The water was clear and refreshing. As evening approached, we fished fresh shrimp bait with hand lines for hardheads.

In the fall and winter, every creek produced yellow perch and pike of record-contending size. Twelve to sixteen foot bamboo poles with float bobbers and brass spreaders and baited with live bull minnow was the rig of choice. You quietly rowed to your favorite fishing spot. Outboard motors were for the summer folks.

Winter brought out the gill and fyke nets. White and yellow perch to 12 inches were not uncommon. Large menhaden called "Bug Fish" were turned into farm compost by the hundreds of pounds per net. The Bug Fish were so named because of gill lice on almost all those six inches or larger.

Ice signaled trapping season for muskrat.

It meant checking your trap run before going to school in the morning and setting the traps by lantern light after other chores. You got to know every tidal swamp and cove. Every humic of grass that would support your weight. You got to know where not to step so as to avoid sinking into the freezing mud. After school, you would skin the 'rats' and stretch the hide. The meat was not wasted. A good season would produce 75 to 100 hides sold at $1.25 to $3.00 per hide. It may not seem like much money now, but as a teen with no other income, it became a windfall for the family.

The first locust blooming in the spring meant the first crab run. The trot lines with carefully preserved baits of eel or tripe were set on a favorite bar drop-off. Beds of grass produced doublers, peelers, and soft crabs. We stood in the bows of our rowboats and poled ourselves along with long-handled soft crab nets. The water was clear enough to follow an escaping crab at depths of five feet. We knew special hiding places that would produce a soft crab at each outgoing tide. It was a sure thing, just poke your net under a rock or root and out one comes. It was not uncommon to catch a dozen or two in an hour of outgoing tide. Good money at 50 cents a dozen.

Among the grass were countless nesting circles of the sunfish each pair fanning tails to clear the sand and grass for their nest. An acceptable procedure was to place a crab net on the bottom over the nesting place. The sunnys, though scared away, would cautiously return to their nest, only to be trapped in a quickly raised net. Proud but unknowing, we would yell, "I got two more."

Gone now are the grass beds with the shed-ding crab, the nesting sunny, the hungry pike and yellow perch. Gone are the quiet evenings with hand lines and hardheads. Gone are the clear wa-ter, the cane pole, the spreader and the quiet peace while waiting for the telltale tug on the bobber. Gone are the muskrat and their domed lodges, the cattails, reeds, and quiet ponds. Gone are my young memories of better times and places. Who is to blame? I share a burden of guilt.

Guilt for inflicting damage on that won-derful, sensitive ecosystem. The crabs, the fish, the muskrat were all there for the taking. We did not realize our damaging actions and their effect on the future. We were part of the river's degradation.

Capt. John E. Rothamel

ON OCTOBER 29,1991, THE SKIPJACK SIGSBEE SINKS OFF SANDY POINT LIGHT. Her 'push boat' was the only part not salvaged from the bottom and it is a visual form of regulation. It ensures that no means of power can be used while dredging oysters under sail. The small motor boat is simply lifted from the water.

> *"When you do your best, that's all you can do"*
>
> Daniel Beck

"KEEPERS OF THE BAY"

Fiction by Steve Burch

It was eight-thirty on a Saturday morning and retired Captain Lester had agreed the night before to take his four-year old grandson Danny and his five-year old granddaughter Taylor down to Mike's old grocery store. This was the arena where Lester would beat his retired first mate "Peacoat" at dominoes and end Peacoat's three-week winning streak.

Truth be told, he didn't mind playing Captain for the day with his grandchildren. Their mother, Celia, and their grandmother, Amelia, needed to drive up to the city and see about getting an old air-conditioner repaired. Without the children the women could go about their business and stop for some relaxed shopping and lunch. Amelia especially loved treating herself to a mid-afternoon root beer float down at Barry's Ice Cream Parlor. Besides, if truth were to be told, the Captain loved both Danny and Taylor, and he really enjoyed their company and their questions. He also had a score to settle with Peacoat.

BALTIMORE COUNTY
Back Neck River

Peacoat was named not for his preferred winter apparel, though no one could remember seeing him wear anything else but the same dark navy peacoat for the last forty years. He was called Peacoat because that was his name. At least in English. His mother, Marie Picot, had been born on the island of St. Pierre off the Grand Banks of Canada where her father was a doryman. Marie had come down to the Bay as a young woman to teach school and had met a handsome and imaginative waterman, Tom Morgan, whom she married. Their one and only son (they also had five daughters) she named after her father, Jacques Picot, which quickly became Jack Peacoat, and finally the first name was dropped as it was no longer necessary. Everyone on the Bay knew Peacoat.

After the women drove off, Captain

"Eels are crazy. You don't find 'em, you just bump into each other."

Bill Lampkins

Lester and the children marched along the worn down path that skirted several backyards and a few grave markers to the harbor and the store. It was late August, yet Captain Lester thought he detected a slight chill in the air. He wondered if this meant autumn would arrive early.

When the trio arrived at Mike's store Peacoat was sitting at the card table, scratching at his stubbly chin and tapping his box of dominoes, ready to get down to business, while Mike, the proprietor, was brewing up some coffee.

"Hi, kids," called out Peacoat. "Ready to watch me beat your old grandpa?'

"No way," replied Taylor defiantly, "he's gonna win today." "Yeah!" agreed Danny.

Captain Lester shrugged and smiled. "My cheerleaders."

Mike brought over the two steaming mugs of coffee, placed them by each contestant's left elbow, and beckoned to the children, "Come over to the counter," where he had some chocolate milk already poured.

As the two players set up their pieces, Mike winked at Peacoat and asked Lester,

"You send that letter?"

"I did," he replied. The Captain took a deep breath and waited for Peacoat to say something argumentative. But Peacoat was seemingly preoccupied with his dominoes.

"What letter did you send, Grampa?" asked Danny.

Mike, Danny, and Taylor crossed to the card table and pulled up three chairs to form a spectators' gallery. Taylor was five and had no trouble with her chair. Danny, who was four, still needed a box to sit on.

"Your grandfather wrote to his congressman in Washington," Mike explained.

"Our congressman," Lester corrected. Peacoat snorted, but the Captain chose to ignore it for

HARVESTING EELS. 19 year-old Eddie Ford has been working the Bay since he was six and going out with his waterman father. "You can go eeling with us anytime, but if you go 10,000 times it will be the same process as today. Hopefully, though, next time we'll fill that box for you."

the moment. He continued his explanation, "Somebody had to do it. We had our Watermen's Association meeting last month, and it just struck me that all we was doin' was belly-achin'. So I wrote. And sent it." Captain Lester looked at his friends and sadly shook his head.

Peacoat grinned. "Well I'm glad you did it. While you was getting all riled and steamed, I was studyin' my domino strategy." He rubbed his large

"Why do men stay with a profession whose future looks fickle at best? The answer lies in part with the challenge."

George C. Carey

weathered hands together and arched his eyebrows.

"What was in the letter, Grampa?" asked Danny.

"It was about the problems we're all having with these new regulations on fishing the Bay," explained Mike. Wanting to be helpful, he added, "You see, kids, we have all kinds of fishermen here."

"We got a lot of people who think they're fishermen," Captain Lester scoffed as Peacoat nodded vigorously.

Taylor scrunched up her face. "But they're not fishermen?"

"Some of them are," Mike replied, as he thoughtfully stroked his walrus-sized moustache. "But they're not watermen. You see, some are part of the Bay, like Peacoat and your daddy and grandfather. Some are not."

Peacoat turned his hawklike profile and faced the children. "And some just think because they got some new and expensive types of gear, that they can be watermen. Only they don't know what they're all about."

Lester continued, "People comin' in to fish, they figure they're a little smarter than us locals, see. They've got a little better idea. They're gonna do it easier, and it's gonna work better."

"Everybody thinks they're smarter than the average commercial waterman," snorted Peacoat. "The problem isn't new gear. Or even how it gets used. The problem is the government and the scientist who have a political agenda. because they all been to school, got a diploma and read a lot of books, and make too much money. They figure, because they can afford it, that they know the Bay better than we do. How do they expect us to trust a man who doesn't work with his hands? They think the problem is us. But the real problem is the thirteen and one-half million people flushin' their toilets and sprayin' chemicals on their lawns and farms. It all ends up in the Chesapeake, and it makes her sick."

A silence descended on the room as the three men sat and thought about their anger. After several moments, Peacoat laid down the first domino and the game began. Taylor watched the patterns grow along the table and then remembered something she had seen on her father's boat.

"Grampa, do you watch your machine finder? You know, to find fish?"

"That's called a depth finder, darlin'," and Captain Lester rubbed her head.

Peacoat snorted, "I think everybody's fully lookin' at their depth finders and everybody's always seein' something. Could be sea nettles, could be a winch head, or might be striped bass." Peacoat stopped playing for a moment and looked at the children. "Probably just seein' their own fool reflections in the glass."

"It depends on where you are," Mike stroked his well-waxed moustache, "what time of the year, and what's happening. Every day's a different day. The wind changes, the tide changes, the salinity changes. Heck, where is the food the fish eat? It all makes a difference, and it all changes every hour of every day, and you got to be looking

TRAPPING CATFISH ON THE BUSH RIVER WITH FYKE NETS. The National Fisheries Institute reports that catfish is the sixth most consumed fish in the U.S.

at more than just your machines." Mike refilled the coffee and the chocolate milks. "And you know, drift net fishing, it's just not the efficient piece of gear everybody thinks it is," he offered. "The fish know it and sense it when it's there. They got to be excited, gotta be feeding and running, and get pushed into the net. You know that your daddy and the others aren't allowed to fish at night like your grandpa used to."

Peacoat grunted, "Daylight hours, man-made hours. Not to the tide, not to the bay. Like fish work nine to five. I can remember down on the Potomac fishing the shad and herring runs with my Dad, when the river looked like little cit-

"Cap'n, it's a job; it is work. You come home at night and your arms hurt so bad–I've had my arms hurting so bad I'd hang them over the side of the bed. That's the only way I could stop them from hurting."

Adolph Welch

ies at night. Light dancing on the water like pretty girls at a party. The men living in arks, fishing the tide".

Mike continued, "There's a lot of propaganda about how the Bay's been ruined and overfished."

"What's proppa-what?" Taylor wanted to know.

"Propaganda," answered Captain Lester. "That's where you say an opinion about something over and over and nobody gets to hear a different opinion, and it gets said so much that everyone believes it."

"Well, actually, you can propagandize

HARVESTING A POUND NET ON THE SUSQUEHANNA FLATS. "A Pound Net is a stationary trap formed of nets supported on stakes. It consists of several sections of netting, including the pound head, an enclosure of small meshed net with a netting floor, a funnel leading into the head, the false pound, a heart-shaped enclosure, and the leader, or hedging, a straight wall of netting from the pound head to the shore. As fish swim along the shore, they are turned into the pound by the leader, and are finally trapped in the pound head."

Paula J. Johson

"Pound Netting has been good to me. I love this. It's a good way to make a living: good, honest work. Life's riches take many forms."

Henry 'Pip' Pratt

HARFORD COUNTY
Susquehanna Flats

facts as well as opinions," Mike corrected.

"Sure, I know that," Captain Lester admitted, "but all everybody hears about is how the Bay is being spoiled by greed."

Peacoat broke in. "It's a good clean fishery that's got a bad rep because of what happens when the water gets polluted."

As Captain Lester slowly sipped his coffee, Danny looked up and asked, "So what did you say in your letter, Grampa?"

Captain Lester looked at his friends and at his grandchildren. He put down his mug and spread open his wide calloused hands.

"What I said was that there were too many boats in the fishing area, too many people, too many nets running over each other. I said there's different kinds of fish to be found in different parts of the Bay, but never in the same place all the time. I said you can't accurately predict the Bay with fancy computers and slide rulers. They don't have the records, they have just started to do the research, and most of all they don't have 'the knowing' that people who have lived the Bay for generations have."

Peacoat angrily slapped his palm down on the table. "There ought to be a law against all them pretty recreational boats! They should tell **them** when and where and how they can play with their expensive toys, regulate **them**. For **them** it's just an inconvenience when they rip up a line of crab pots or run through my pound net. For me, I'm trying to feed my family."

"But this is America," objected Mike. "You can't tell people how to do it, not by law you can't. Each individual's got to learn for themselves what's important. Everybody's got to do it. Even Danny and Taylor got to learn for themselves."

Lester evenly regarded his first mate and partner and agreed, "so why not educate them?"

"Who? The politicians?" Peacoat snorted, "I heard once of a politician who fell into a snake pit. The snakes never bit him. And you know why?" He grinned and looked slyly at his friends, "professional courtesy!"

The Captain and Mike laughed, but the Captain continued his thought, "yeah, but they're not the enemy. Come on, Peacoat, every politician starts out by wantin' to help his neighbor. Only that neighbor hasn't been us. But that's what they do in the legislature. They help people. But usually only those that can speak clearly and make their point."

"You mean yell with money in the bank," objected Peacoat.

Lester dropped all pretense of playing the game and spread open his hands and looked directly at Peacoat. "Sure, sometimes money is the grease in the wheel. But only sometimes. You can go out and buy yourself a pretty little boat — a real one, I'm saying, not just one for show — and you can rig it proper with all the right gear. The best netting, spare nothing. But all that and the best charts and training, I mean, there are no stop signs on the bay that say 'stop here and catch fish'. Only the understanding that comes from having to make a living everyday will teach you that. How are you going to work the Bay or even understand her without learning what we learned when we was little boys watching and listening to the older watermen down the store when they was playing dominoes? How are you going to learn about different tides, and which banks can be worked at which times of the day, the month, the year, or the season? Politicians and scientists and the media all have the tools to learn, but they don't have the years of listening to know. Of listening and going out on the Chesapeake and lookin' with their own eyes and learning the truth. Of listening to her speak.

"You see," the Captain continued, "These old watermen, their knees are all bad, and they're too old to go out each day and work with the younger fellows. They was our schoolmasters, our teachers, and what they gave us — the same way it was given to them — was a seminar about how to learn from the Chesapeake herself. It was the true learning, the knowing, that's what it was. Their store was our schoolhouse and their stories, the older watermen's stories, those stories was our lessons. Do you know another schoolhouse with the smells of hemp, coffee, salt, wood, fish and tobacco? I can remember my mother sniffin' my fingers and my hair and complaining to Uncle Buddy that I smelled like a saloon! And that school was also our recess, our playground. Imagine! Penny candies instead of chalk. Baseball on the radio and stories on how to cull oysters.

"And when we was old enough to join our daddies and our older brothers out on the Bay, when we began our apprenticeship with them, why we came with our heads and our hearts full of the learning that makes a waterman out of a young boy. The stories that were and are passed down from generation to generation — for over three hundred years — these have made educated men out of every waterman who works and harvests the Chesapeake Bay."

Peacoat would not be silenced! "I understand what you're saying," he conceded, "I even learned the same way from my daddy, and he even told me stories 'bout bein' out on the ocean once up by the Grand Banks with my grandpa. But what I'm saying is when you see somebody coming down on you and they're not used to fishin', and their waves almost knock you overboard, how you goin' to educate them? Call them on the radio or go tell them? Watermen here, sportsmen there? What kind of a solution is that?"

Suddenly Peacoat furiously scratched his scalp, grunted, and continued, "Or maybe tellin' us that we can crab for jimmies on some days and sooks on others? Then what do we do when the weather don't let us? What do we do when we're not working from the same page? You know, it's not hard to slip down the ladder. You work with the same government man for years, come to understand each other, work in the right direction. Then you know what happens? We get a new elected government, one that sees the Chesapeake as a park, not as a breeder of living things. All that water is for things to grow and die in and not just look at. It's the beauty underneath that makes her adorable.

"And how about the Susquehanna River and all its runoff? The river runs all the way down from Cooperstown in New York state and brings with it all the sewage treatment and the strip mines and the farm chemicals and dumps it into our Bay! How are a bunch of lawyers and stock-brokers in the legislature going to understand a man who works in a natural environment? They go to their eight-hour-a-day jobs in their new cars that keep the rain from their expensive suits, and they go into their offices and look out the window and say to themselves 'what nasty weather we're havin'." Peacoat rose and walked over to the door, looking out across the inlet. His hands shook with frustration.

"But we can't work those days. And those days don't always fall on the days someone in the legislature determined that none of us are supposed to work. The Fourth of July is a great holiday and everybody gets the day off, right? Only the crabs don't know it's a holiday, so we work. And now? 'Cause someone reported that the crab count is down, never mind that no one knows why yet, they passed a law telling us we can't fish no more. And it happens overnight. We wake up to a nice cup of coffee and a ban on fishing; it all happens too quick. But we make our living knowin' the Bay; it's what feeds our children, and we don't want it fished out either!"

Peacoat returned from the door to face his friends. "We are not the enemy here! My daddy told me we was the Keepers of the Bay, not its enemy! So, Captain, my friend, what is the answer? What did you suggest to Representative what's-his-name?"

Peacoat moved to his seat and leaned his chair against Mike's Community Bulletin Board, where Mary Cobb had just posted the announcement of the birth of her third granddaughter, Alice, 7 lbs. 3 oz.

"I don't know the answers," Captain Lester replied. "I honestly don't know. I think everybody is wishing we had a system. But there's always going to be people that think they deserve more. There's always going to be that."

The men and children waited for the Captain to finish his thought.

"So I wrote to our congresspersons. All of them. I told them, or tried to, about what we do here on the Chesapeake, that we're a community. Or we should be, Peacoat. I want them to know what's happening here because of their regulations. Regulations on the days we fish, regulations on what kind of gear we use. They regulate and never listen to our input, what we know about what we do. They got the tools and the power to help. But they got to understand. Somehow we got to educate them.

"Just like us, Grampa?" Danny inquired.

Taylor's face set in a serious mood, and she looked straight at her grandfather and the other men and demanded, "Why don't you bring them here and teach them like you're teaching us? Make them go to our school!"

Captain Lester smiled, and he leaned over and hugged his granddaughter. "That's what we're trying, darlin'. And we're not gonna stop trying, 'cause we want the both of you to have this Bay when we're long gone."

Peacoat broke into a smile and patted her head. "Yep, we want you to have what we got." He winked at Danny.

Mike looked over at Peacoat and nodded. "That was a nice thing your Daddy said, Peacoat. I like that. Keepers of the Bay. Yes sir, that's what we are. That's what we've always been."

There was a moment of silence as the older men looked at the children. The men sat and listened to the water outside and thought about when they were children. They remembered their fathers and grandfathers, and they remembered the bountiful harvest of their Bay. Without a word, without anyone asking, Mike offered the children an unheard of third glass of chocolate milk. Then Peacoat and the Captain realized that they couldn't remember whose turn it was. So Mike declared the game a draw. Both men had won.

Steve Burch

"Nature is a successful model of many things that human communities seek: continuity, stability and sustenance, adaptation, sustained productivity, diversity and evolutionary change."

Joeseph Sax

"You need to have faith in two things: time and nature."

KENT COUNTY
Rockhall

*"Fame is vapor, popularity an accident, riches take wings.
Only one thing endures and that is character."*
Horace Greeley

AGENTS OF CONSEQUENCE

*"Lawmakers must realize over-regulating
the Bay can corrode communities"*

Article by Karen J. Rohr

Situated a solid two hours' drive from
Baltimore, MWA President Larry Simns' town of
Rockhall is on the Eastern Shore of the Bay. Here,
people still wave as they drive past one another.

Not a big wave.

Just a slight raise of the hand from the
steering wheel. A subtle movement, carrying with
it a great deal of respect.

"The media makes the crab situation
more urgent than it actually is," Simns explains as
the murmur of watermen's voices rises and falls
around him in the local gathering place — a small
restaurant warm with the smell of coffee, pan-
cakes, and sausage.

"The media manages too much information. The public wants instant gratification and
they get it." Simns may have a point.

The Baltimore Sun in August 1995 published the Chesapeake Bay Foundation's proposal for proactive management of the blue crab. The proposal involved a "blue crab sanctuary" to stabilize the "highly variable catches" of the last few years. Phrases such as "perilously close to collapse," "emergency rescue plan", and a "crisis can be avoided" littered the article. The sanctuary sought to ban the harvest in waters below 40 feet in the Maryland and Virginia portions of the Bay.

"We estimate it would close approximately 25% of the tidal waters in the main Bay and its tributaries and provide protection for about 50 percent of the mature female component of the crab population," according to the foundation's proposal. The plan clearly targets commercial crabbers. This despite the assertion by foundation fisheries scientist Bill Goldsborough that his group's interest is in the conservation of crabs as opposed to allocation of regulations to stabilize the crab population.

Though implementation of the plan would have a devastatingly negative impact on the watermen's lives, the foundation did not formally consult with the watermen for input before going public with the proposal.

"The ebb and flow of animal populations in Maryland creates natural imbalances that are not always easy to resolve."

Tom Horton

Harley Speir, Department of Natural Resources biologist, doesn't question the motives, but he questioned the logic behind the proposal.

"How do you account for the tide when it rises above the 40-foot mark? How many crabs live under this 40-foot mark? And how many crabs would the sanctuary actually save?" he asks.

Speir intimates that the political climate, combined with scientific data supporting the instability of the crab population, has hastened regulation of the crab population and the commercial blue crab harvest. Actions taken to control the fishery in the fall of 1995 included regulating the numbers of hours a crabber could work on the water, limiting the number of crab pots to 300 per person per boat, limiting entry into the industry, and cutting the 1995 season short by about a month. Yet "sorting out the effects these regulations have on the crab populations is next to impossible," Speir admits.

It seems the regulations' impacts on the watermen are more measurable.

Simns says the rules resulted in the loss of jobs for people harvesting crabs, as well as for people on the shore who maintain the crab-catching gear and unload the boats. Furthermore, abbreviating the crab season upsets the balance between crab and oyster season, a situation nearly unique to Rockhall, as oysters remained healthy there. Usually, the crab season tapers off slowly as some watermen begin to harvest oysters in the fall, and because these seasons overlap, there is a gradual change in the fishing pressure on oysters. This abrupt change over hurt the oystermen and the crabbers.

"Management should never be fast. A long-range plan would have been much better," Simns said.

Speir, a 20-year employee, says there is "a priority to involve the watermen in the process." The Blue Crab Steering Committee, formed in 1993, brings together watermen, scientists, and DNR and Chesapeake Bay Foundation representatives and offers input to the management plan for the crab.

Active on the committee, Simns is dedicated to his way of life and to the watermen he represents.

In 1970 or so, Simns recalls going to Annapolis to wrangle over legislation affecting the watermen. He's been the president of the Maryland Watermen's Association ever since. The group provides a networking tool for the watermen and gives the commercial fishermen a voice in the bureaucracies affecting the fisheries.

In the beginning Simns volunteered for the MWA, but eventually he told the group he had to step down as president because the post was consuming too much of his valuable fishing time. The group wanted him to stay, and they found the funds to pay him part-time. Even though being president is still not cost effective, Simns doesn't do it for the pay: "It's a hard juggling act, but it's rewarding."

His main concern of late has been negotiating blue crab fisheries policies that are acceptable to the watermen and are supported by scientific evidence.

"We want specific data from the scientists before the policies are agreed upon," Simns said. But specific data is just what is lacking.

What is over-fishing? How many crabs do recreational crabbers catch? How many crabs are found in SAV areas? A list of as-yet-unanswered questions spout from the heading "Research Needs" in the Blue Crab Management Plan. Even Speir admits, "We have no good handle on the population prediction."

Until this laundry list of questions is answered, there is no way of creating equitable fisheries regulations. Regulations have a direct cause and effect on the economic survival of the watermen and their families. And erring on the side of heavy-handed regulations can be as damaging as being too light-handed. The people of Rock Hall know just how devastating the mismanagement of a fisheries can be.

In 1985, the moratorium placed on striped bass permanently altered the town. Processing plants and ice plants revolving around the striped bass industry closed. People lost jobs. Former plant sites along the shoreline were purchased by developers and transformed into expensive docking areas — areas outside the affordability of watermen. Condominiums were built adjacent to watermen's modest homes, sending property taxes soaring to heights that forced watermen to struggle to hold on to their homes. And young people could no longer depend on the fishing industry to give them a future.

Simns even says Rock Hall has become a place for almost any drug desired. "The young people want fast money in their pockets. Used to be that the fishery could take care of that. But not anymore."

These days, imposing regulations intended to conserve a species in the Bay means slow erosion of a community landside. Thus is life for a waterman in the mid-1990s.

Karen J. Rohr

"Historically, family was the thing that succored us, the last line of defense against the machinations of the world."

Leonard Pitts Jr.

"You know, when you're out there on the
water, on Miss Jeanne, and you got the
engine running and the patent tong motor
running, and it's up and down, the tong
pullin' a lick, pullin' a lick.

"And you're cullin' for all your worth,
trying to catch your limit before three
o'clock, there's not much you can do,
you know, with your mind except...
think.

"Like... what you did twenty years ago,
and you should have done different, or
about your kids, or about the Bay.
Or, this thought, which just came over
me once. When you're on God's culling
board, are you box or are you cull?"

Hudson 'Huddie' Swann,
Oysterback Waterman

Soft Shell Clamming

with Hydraulic Dredge

"It's too hot, too noisy, and it stinks,"

was how Emma Boulter described soft shell clamming with her Dad. For me, working around the hydraulic dredge was like Lucille Ball and Vivian Vance in the chocolate factory. Upon which a great water-belching beast erupts from the deep to have a rock picked from its teeth.

"In 1972, Maryland's clam industry was dealt a severe blow when Hurricane Agnes swept through the region, covering the soft shell clam beds with tons of silt and fresh water. In addition to the devastation of Agnes, other factors have contributed to the general decline of the clam industry. Poor water quality, disease, and rapid siltation in some areas have caused clam die-offs and, consequently, a temporarily closed fishery, as in 1984. Over-harvesting, made simple with the efficient hydraulic dredge, is another possible factor in the decline of soft clam populations."

Paula J. Johson

CHESAPEAKE BAY FACTS
AND A NOTE ABOUT KENT ISLAND PIRACY

Some of which are even true

The origin of the name Chesapeake comes from the Indian term for "Great Shellfish Growing Water", and its most famous mythological inhabitant is Chessie, a lady cousin to the Loch Ness monster. The Bay is the largest estuary in the nation with a surface area of 4,400 square miles. Her rivers and creeks drain six states and 27 million toilets.

There is enough tidal shoreline to stretch across the country nearly three times, of which only 160 miles can be walked on without trespassing.

The Chesapeake Bay is 190 miles long and holds 18 trillion gallons of water. According to Willie Poag of the U.S. Geological Survey, "the basin that would eventually become the Chesapeake Bay was created by an asteroid or comet collision 35 million years ago. That impact left a crater 50 miles across, with ground zero at a site that is now Cape Charles."

The Bay as we know it was formed 11,000 years ago when the rising seas caused by melting glaciers (global warming?), flooded the Susquehanna River valley.

There are many duplicate names for the Chesapeake's rivers and creeks. There are four Back Rivers, six Broad Creeks, three Church Creeks, five Deep Creeks, five Hunting Creeks, four Island Creeks, four Jones Creeks, eight Mill Creeks, three Northwest Branches, four Oyster Creeks, four Sandy Points, three Town Points, and four Wicomico Rivers.

Her average depth is 21 feet and she supports two different plant communities: benthic algae and phytoplankton. The salt marshes along the shoreline of the Chesapeake can produce 10 tons of organic matter per acre per year (the average yield of domestic wheat is only 1½ tons).

Donald Shomette claims that the first documented act of piracy on the Chesapeake was the seizure of a trading vessel and its cargo in 1635 for invading the trading dominion of Kent Island.

Oyster 'Shaft' or 'Hand' tongs are rake-like tools on wood shafts used to collect oysters off the bottom of creeks and rivers. They are the simplest and oldest type of oystering gear, and the most widely used.

The Straight Facts about Providing Seafood for the World's Table:

A message from the National Fisheries Institute

Popular Perception:

Commercial fishermen's gill nets are destroying the fishery and should be banned.

Reality:

Initiatives supported by recreational fishing groups to outlaw the use of commercial fishing gear in many state waters such as Maryland are veiled "conservation" efforts that would, in reality, allocate the fish stocks to recreational fishermen only and do nothing to protect the fishery resource. While recreational fishermen may outnumber commercial fishermen, the select number of fishermen who work the waters for a living are the servants of the consumer who cannot catch their own seafood.

"Pollution, profits, people, and politics will determine the future"

R. J. Holt

QUEEN ANNES COUNTY
Kent Island

"Anything he did, he thought I should be able to do it to. My husband and I are working toward the same goal, and we are working together to make it happen. That's what's attractive about it."

Karen Lassahn

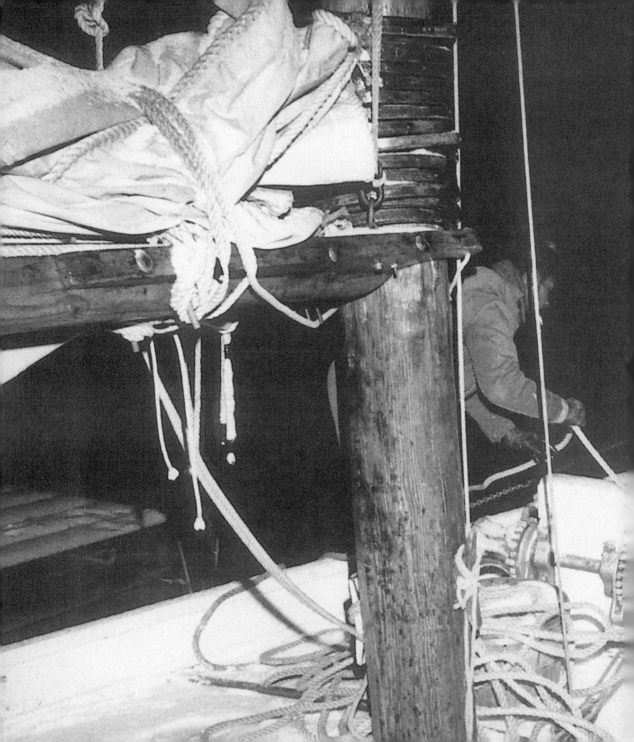

DREDGING OYSTERS
Under Sail

"Nothing's ever warm on the skipjacks,

except when you're painting them in summer. But when there's plenty of oysters, nothing much but ice stops her from going out."

Captain Russell Dize

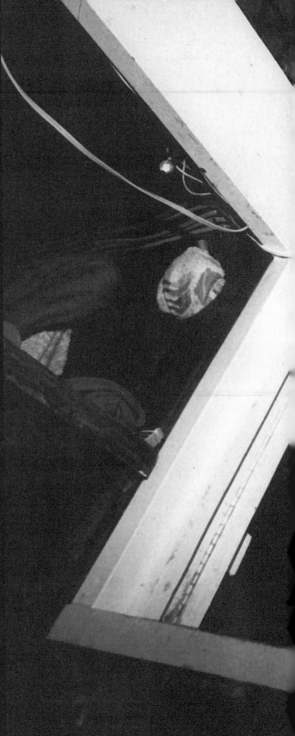

PREACHER: "Are you afraid of going to hell?"

WATERMAN:

"Naw, Reverend, them oyster drudgers tore
that place down long ago."

Across the Knapps Narrows there once was a **HEEL TRUN-NION ROLLING LIFT BRIDGE** with a counter-weight above the roadway. It was Maryland's only overhead counter-weight bridge. The 'Heel Trunnion' refers to the lift mechanism and the fact that it is at the rear of the bridge, not the front. It is now on display at the St. Michaels Maritime Museum — who'd ever have thought about a bridge park?

TALBOT COUNTY
Tilghman

Dispatches from the Mythical
Town of Oysterback

Fiction from The Oysterback Tales
by Hellen Chapple

CUCUMBER NIGHT will be August 25th this year, Mrs. Nettie Leery says. Join your neighbors in leaving all those thousands of cukes that have suddenly appeared in your garden on the doorsteps of your neighbors in the dead of the night! This year bluefish and excess tomatoes will also be included in the fun.

OYSTERBACK MIDDLE SCHOOL art teacher Griselda Everdean will present her student dance troupe, Ballet Folklorico de Tilghman Island, in a performance at the Community Center. Ms. Everdean will solo in her acclaimed "Dance de Defiance aux Jesse Helms."

THE BIG EXCITEMENT last week was the Oysterback High School Reunion, held at the Oysterback High School. The Boone Brothers, Mike and Gabe, Class of '68, showed up, surprising many people, since they have not been seen since 1969. Asked where they'd been and what they'd been doing all these years, Mike Boone said they'd been living off the land. Finding out the Vietnam War was over in 1975, they decided they might stick around and open a fix-it shop over to Tubman's Corners where the old gas station used to be. Gabe says if you can remember the sixties, you probably weren't there.

"Think that we might end up losing the bay, not to water pollution or toxic chemicals, but to sameness and tameness, to disconnection."

Tom Horton

The Dance
of fluid Dynamics

18 trillion gallons of fluid swirling in a shallow valley created by melting ice and an asteroid. 14 headwater streams, fresh from the west, doing a 4-step seasonal waltz with the salty ocean. The musical movement of tides, complex but predictable, are the manifestations of the moon. Salt dominates and light penetrates.

Facts About the Chesapeake Bay Watershed

U.S. Fish and Wildlife Service and The USDA Soil Conservation Service

A person 6 feet tall could wade over 700,000 acres of the Bay and barely get the rim of his or her hat wet. These vast shallow areas are ideal places for aquatic plants to grow, as well as excellent spawning and nursery grounds for many bay animals.

Nearly 20 miles long and 20 miles wide, the bay is only 21 feet deep on the   average. Being this shallow means that the bay holds a relatively small volume of water.

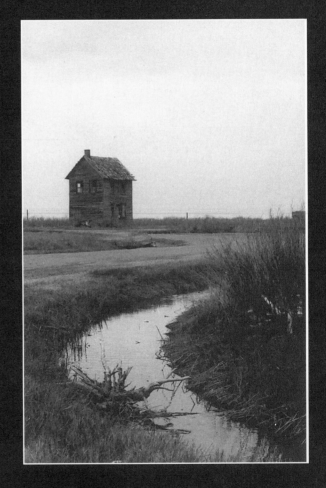

Lawns cover more area in Maryland than corn, the state's largest agricultural crop. Acre for acre, more chemicals are applied to lawns than most agricultural crops.

There are over 100,000 miles of streams and rivers in the Chesapeake watershed. Even though all of us can't see the bay, virtually everyone in the watershed is within a fifteen minute walk of a stream that flows into the bay.

It took until 1950 for the population in the bay watershed to reach 6 million. By 1990, 40 years later, the population more than doubled to over 13 million, and is expected to surpass 16 million by 2020.

"Only when we understand how our daily routines affect the Bay can we restore its productivity and preserve its beauty."

DORCHESTER COUNTY
Hoopers Island

"GIRLY JOB"

Fiction by Steve Burch

The Bay was choppy and the clouds scudded across the sky on an early March morning. The island ferry handled the water with its customary ease for the forty-minute voyage, but Kelly Jordan spent the entire trip in a disturbed state, wondering, as the occasional wave splashed across the bow, if the boat would sink. She also had occasion to wonder about the indigestible donut she had wolfed down as she raced to catch the boat; and whether it would soon be seen from the side railing among the choppy waters.

When incipient seasickness and fear of drowning weren't crowding her mind, she tried to imagine seeing her Aunt Karen and Uncle Jesser Lesher and their thirteen-year-old daughter Pauli (Pauline) and what she would say to them and, more importantly, what they would say to her. Her mother's tearful and angry "What am I going to do with you?" burned in her ears, and Kelly's skinny frame filled with resentment — against her mother, against her alternate-weekends father, against her so-called friends who wouldn't or couldn't stick up for her. If Aunt Karen thought she could lecture Kelly just like the others and turn against her when she needed a friend, well she certainly would find out in one quick hurry how fast Kelly would stay on this stupid island in the middle of No Place, U.S.A.

Captain Jasper (who Kelly remembered was supposed to be someone she was related to, but wasn't sure if he was a cousin or what) skippered the 'ferry boat', **QUEEN OF THE ISLAND**. The **QUEEN** was a 40x14 fishing boat whose main cargo consisted of passengers, mail, and groceries for the islanders. As it bounced across the waves, its current consignment remained securely lashed behind ropes: crates of vegetables, cases of sodas and paper products, boxes of canned goods. Cabbages shared the space with a crated, newly bought washing machine, weighted down with a truck tire perched atop.

Most of its nine passengers sat in the 10'x14' cabin with the Captain. Two middle-aged women talked animatedly about a horror movie recently seen on the mainland, a recently widowed woman dozed behind a Harlequin romance novel, and one young mother, who had both a toddler and an infant in tow, was conversing on a cellular phone. A teenage girl sat inside, reading a magazine, while a girlfriend braided her long blonde hair; and a thirty-ish man in a civilian uniform stood at the rail, deep in thought, as if only here could he find his private space. Seated next to Kelly in the open rear of the boat was a nine-year old boy whose down jacket remained open to reveal a T-shirt that read, "I may be little, but to God I'm Big Stuff."

Gradually, a pencil-thin line of amber

green began to delineate the horizon, and Kelly knew that the island was near. She spotted a house on the starboard side, sitting alone on a spit of land, seemingly isolated from the world itself. The boat passed a series of markers, poles with large green squares with odd numbers attached to them. On one a large nest resided, but its occupant was nowhere in sight. As they got closer, the spit of land turned out to be an island engulfed by eelgrass. The house was abandoned, chalk-white with broken windows and rusted oil drums in its rear. Cormorants appeared to live in the house now, and they could be seen silently observing the passing boat.

"I could live there," thought Kelly. "Away from everything and everyone. Just me and the sound of the wind and the water." She gazed at the house with a renewed and ferocious energy, thinking of herself at her mother's age, living alone, silent and remote. Not like her real mother, though. Always nagging, always yelling — at her, at her father, at her friends: never satisfied.

The clouds began to increase in quantity as the **QUEEN OF THE ISLAND** slowly chugged past a pair of dredges in the channel between the islands. As it pulled into the docking area the winds became gusty. Kelly looked across the mini gravel parking lot and was greeted by a large wave from Aunt Karen, standing alone next to her battered sky-blue golf cart. "Why is she smiling?" thought Kelly, "and where are the others? Where's Pauli?"

Kelly picked up her duffel bag and ambled off the boat and into Karen's strong and smoky kisses. Without even a word asked, Karen adroitly shifted Kelly's bag onto her own shoulder and led the eleven-year-old across the planked dock as Jasper and his crew began the process of unloading the supplies. They climbed in the cart, and before starting the motor, Karen lit a cigarette, then wordlessly offered the pack to Kelly, who just shook her head.

"Great," Karen enthused, "maybe Pauli could learn from you that you don't have to smoke to be cool. Though I'll tell you a little secret." Karen smiled as Kelly glanced over her shoulder at her aunt. "Your mother and me was advised to smoke by our daddy. Yep, that's right, your grandfather. Said if we was gonna be workin' on the Bay, we're gonna be smellin' nothing but fish. Said smokin' helped cut down on the assault to the nose. And you know, I hate to admit that he was right. A filthy, disgusting habit, but the old man was right."

Karen guffawed at the memory as she started up the cart and slowly puttered on toward her home at the other end of the island. Kelly hoped that Karen was in a good mood and would not notice that her passenger was leaning out over the side of the cart to cut down on the assault to her nose by her aunt's smelly cigarette.

As she idly gazed along the narrow winding lanes (they couldn't be thought of as streets, though they were named streets), Kelly reflected on the photos her mother kept of a flat landscape dotted with one or two story houses, some of them little better than shacks, none of them looking under twenty-five years old. Each yard was overflowing with traps, buoys, ropes, and junkyard cars on cinder blocks, to be cannibalized for parts to keep the slightly newer cars from completely breaking down.

But the houses she saw weren't shacks and were far from depressed. Granted there were few that were under twenty-five years old, but they were kept in good condition, solid and comfortable. The lanes crisscrossed each other in a dense grid, each house occupying a tiny plot of ground. Yet there was a sense of room enough, occupants sensing the needs of their neighbors, unlike the city where a sense of lives spilling over into others' seemed to abound.

Kelly suddenly realized that Karen had asked her a question. "I'm sorry?"

"As soon as we began to travel faster in this country, the importance of place got lost."

Vine Deloria

"I asked if you saw your father much, or is that kinda personal?" Karen smiled and shook her head, stubbing out her cigarette. "I'm not trying to be nosy. Look, I'll make a deal with you. At any time you can tell me to mind my own business, and that's all it'll take. No more questions. No hard feelings either. What do you say? A deal?"

"A deal."

"Good."

Karen quickly glanced at Kelly to see if there'd be any response, but all she saw was a wordless, expressionless Kelly. In the silence Karen noted several piercings in Kelly's ears and nose, and the preponderance of black in the clothing: jeans, T-shirt hiding under a charcoal grey sweater, and a dark down coat.

"Pauli will be glad to see you."

"Why?" Toneless, without interest.

"'Cause she likes you, silly. She may be two years older, but you live in the city and get to see and do all sorts of neat things. Not like around here. I mean it's good, we like it, but it's an entire way of life that can be pretty unconnected to the mainland's way of life. Certainly unconnected to anything you'll ever see on television."

"How so?"

"It's hard to get away from, there's just too many pretty times."

John Edwards

"'Cause around here, everybody eats, drinks, prays, goes to the bathroom, and does pretty much everything else to the seasons and individual days of the Chesapeake. The Bay runs our lives. Government too. But it's the Bay, always the Bay. Like Jesse and I didn't just marry each other, we married the Bay that's in both of us. Your mother got away from it, it wasn't her kind of life. And I never blamed her. It's awfully hard. It's no nine to five job, leave it at the end of the day, throw back a few beers and forget about it 'til you go to work the next day."

"Here we are."

Karen pulled the cart beside a long, low building smack against the long reed grasses that separated it from the water. Constructed from wood and painted gray with white trim, the Island Ladies' Crabmeat Co-op was the first newish building Kelly had seen since she got off the boat.

"This where you work?"

Karen grinned. "Uh-huh. This is where I 'work'. Come on in and let me show you."

Both women got out of the cart and simultaneously pulled up the collars of their jackets as the temperature suddenly dropped. Karen looked up at the sky and the thickening clouds, then checked her watch. Kelly realized that her aunt had adjusted her smile. Karen walked to the door and opened it.

"Buy you some coffee?"

Without a word or sign, Kelly entered the co-op, and Karen followed. It was warmer, much warmer, and Karen slipped off her coat and hung it on a peg. Kelly slipped hers off and handed it to Karen and took a few tentative steps from the entrance into a large, clean, well-lit room of four long stainless steel tables surrounded by white plastic lawn chairs, each with a woman's name stenciled on its back. On each table were neatly arranged piles of plastic containers, lids and pre-printed adhesive labels. There were stainless steel sinks along the walls, one of which was decorated with several framed documents and photos. At the far end, was a chalkboard with the heading "Today's Reading" and a quotation from the Scripture scrawled underneath.

"You work here?"

"That's what I do most days. Yep. My home away from home."

Karen crossed to one corner where the coffee maker stood and proceeded to pour in some water and switched it on. Kelly watched all this dully. Just another empty room, boring, full of nothing. What was she going to do here for two whole weeks?

"Do they allow you to smoke here?"

"Hah! This here's a gov'ment approved food processin' building. Got rules. Got regulations. Gotta go outside! So what do you think? About this co-op?"

Kelly shrugged. Think? Could there be 'thought' to a place like this? An island like this? This was nothing nowhere. She hated her mother for forcing her to come here. She wanted to cry.

"There's nothing here!" She whined. "I'd get so bored I'd kill myself! Doesn't Pauli ever go nuts here? How can you stand it? How can anyone stand it? Now I know why my mom ran away from here."

Kelly didn't mean to let all this come slipping out. She didn't think she was a particularly cruel girl, and her aunt and uncle had always been good and kind to her, especially after the divorce. "But it is all so oppressive!" She thought. "The flatness of the land, the grayness of the skies and all that Bay between you and..." Kelly looked over to her aunt, who seemed lost in thought.

Karen slowly nodded. "Yeah, I guess it does seem so to someone like yourself."

Kelly stammered a mumbled apology.

"Nope, no sorrys needed nor asked for," Karen replied. "It's a real problem here. We're losing residents every year. Folks moving to the mainland, mostly the young people. Better jobs, better security, a way of life that's not so hard and uncertain. Those of us who've elected to stay and continue what our mommas and daddies did are probably pretty crazy."

Karen again looked out the window and checked the darkening skies. "Tell you something though. This co-op's been a real blessing. You see, our crabmeat's world famous. And while the guys — and not all of' em guys, my own Pauli's out there with them every day she's not in school — while they're out there crabbing, we're back here picking them for market. 'Cause that's our job. We're crab pickers. Your mother was a crab picker once, too, you know, and until we built this place, we used to work out of our homes."

She smiled and continued, "You wanna talk crazy? Try picking crabs in your kitchen alone with nothing but the radio or the TV in the background for company. Or, in the outbuildings sitting at your little table, with the newspaper spread across it, keeping room for the scale too. Try doing that alone, day after day, and see if you don't start talking to a spider in the corner."

"Then why?"

"Because every person you're gonna see on this island has a deep, almost religious love for this place and the work that they do." Karen smiled and looked embarrassed. "Because my husband catches crabs and I pick 'em, that's why. 'Cause if we don't work together, we don't earn enough to survive. Because of being married to each other and married to our way of life.

"It's spiritual, a sense of belonging, a connectedness to each other and to this place. And that's true about everybody who lives and works this Bay, even if we are getting to be fewer and fewer each year. Jesse and me, and Pauli now too, are doing something that's been done for hundreds of years. And that is harvesting what God and the Chesapeake provide us. Something we hope will still be done when Pauli grows up. We pray everyday that there is still a Bay when I'm a grandmother. But the way pollutants are killing off the stock and the way the politicians are killing off our way of life, I don't know."

"Well I do!"

Kelly turned around and was face to face with a tall, imposing, bespectacled woman with grey-streaked, curly blonde hair who removed her parka and stuck a wad of gum into her mouth. "The Bay don't just belong to the watermen, it don't all belong to the sportfishermen, and it don't belong to the environmentalists. Who it does belong to is everyone and everyone has got to learn to share it together, or we're all gonna lose it! Together! Hi, I'm Joyce. And you must be Karen's niece, Kelly?"

"Kelly Mehorter, my sister Linda's girl, is here to stay with us for a couple of weeks, see what we do, and probably learn to appreciate life on the mainland." Karen winked at Kelly, and Kelly extended her hand to Joyce.

"Well," Joyce continued as if uninterrupted, "she's starting at a good place. You want to learn about the island, you start right here. And the first thing you learn is that we don't work no nine to five. You want to know what the watermen's work ethic is? You go home when the work is done, not when the clock says it's done. You want a new pair of shoes? Then you work. It's pretty simple." Suddenly Joyce burst into merry laughter and turned to Karen. "Am I scaring her yet?"

Both women laughed. Kelly felt uncomfortable, like she had wandered into a private conversation. She sensed she was being made fun of and wanted to know why it was funny. And "how could these strange women find anything funny in their lives?" As she thought this, she saw both women wander to the window and look out at the blackening sky.

"When's Uncle Jesse coming back?"

Karen frowned. "Not for another four, five hours, honey. But if he's smart..." She let her answer dangle against the windowpane.

"If they're all smart, they'll be heading back right now," Joyce offered.

"It's dangerous isn't it? Out there? In this weather?"

Karen gently squeezed Kelly's shoulder. "Hon, it can be dangerous every day of the year."

Joyce coughed. "Not like the fishermen up north New England way, who go out on the ocean for days at a time. Our men work close to home and the Bay's got places a boat can hole up and wait out a storm. But the storms can sneak up on you, and the wind is like the devil climbing up and down a pole, and boats have been lost. This Bay's got many personalities, one of them's quite nasty. But it's her magnificence that touches your soul." Joyce smiled. "Don't mind me. I like talking about the Bay and life on the island. I'm the unofficial spokesperson. The one arrested for picking crabs in an unapproved facility. I know that some day I'm going to forgive those two health inspectors and that DNR Police official. You know, it took all my Christian faith from pushing those three men into the Bay. A week's worth of crab picking, confiscated as I got off the ferry. Arrested on the mainland in front of my family. It was not necessary and was very intimidating. I lost a lot of faith in my government, that day.

But I argued and pled and cajoled and screamed and sweet-talked the legislators and the Health Department into helping us. Not that there was anything ever wrong with our product, but we had to fulfill the letter of the law. It took us four years, but we did it, and believe every word I say to you, to them, to any visitor to this island that we here, on this island, have a way of life and a knowing about the Chesapeake that is valuable. And, oh, I talk too much sometimes," as Joyce looked out the window, "and I am still a little bitter. I'm sorry."

Kelly murmured an excuse, picked up her coat, and walked outside, sensing a need for the two women to talk to each other, maybe about the weather. At first, she wandered around the low building, extending her perambulation out to the tall grass that surrounded the co-op. For a moment, she debated whether or not to stay outside, away from these strangers, these women who seemed lost in their own world. Kelly tried to imagine her mother on this island, but she couldn't imagine her mother being so connected to something or someone. A sudden gust of wind nearly

sent her off her feet and settled the matter.

Returning, Kelly encountered a rail-thin teenaged boy nicknamed Spaghetti who, it turned out, worked late afternoons at the co-op steaming crabs before the women began their picking. He was even less conversant than Kelly herself and seemed preoccupied with adjusting the gears on his mountain bike (like there were any mountains overlooking the Bay!), and besides, he seemed to speak only in grunts. Karen and Joyce remained in the large common room. A radio had been turned on, obviously for the weather report and not the music (which seemed to screech from some kind of golden yesterday when every rock musician who cut an album was part of the collective consciousness of America). The women looked up as Kelly entered.

"What's with the weather?" she asked, trying to be friendly.

Joyce shook her head and Karen smiled through clenched teeth, "Gonna be a tight one. You made it just in time."

The silence that greeted Karen's news lasted several minutes. The older women were obviously worried about the weather and the safety of their families working out on the Bay. Kelly wondered if her mother worried, knowing her daughter was out here on this island, then decided

against that. Her mother was too busy and angry
at Kelly's being suspended from school for two
weeks for the incident with the teacher's aide. She
was too busy to even listen to Kelly's side of the
story, in which Kelly was merely defending her
mother's name. No, no one cared to listen. Kelly
had broken the great rule: she dared to be heard
against an adult, to make her feelings matter in
their world.

But that world began to feel curiously
small right now. Uncle Jesse (whom she hadn't
seen in over three years) and her older cousin Pauli (whom she hadn't seen since last Thanksgiving
at her mother's) were out there somewhere, on a
boat, in the rising wind and rain, in the growing
darkness.

"They're gonna be all right, aren't they?"
just slipped out of Kelly's mouth.

"Oh, they are going to be all right. We all
learn from a very young age how to listen to and
understand nature. We have to, or we don't survive. So you got any questions?"

"Maybe a few."

"Fire away. One of us will answer."

"Well, who's the boss here?"

Joyce jumped in. "No one's the boss.
Actually you're looking at a place with fifteen
bosses. Every woman who works here is her own

boss. We share the space, the tables, and probably more gossip about the island than we want to admit. But we got no boss 'cept ourselves. This is a co-op, not a collective." Joyce picked up a stack of labels. "We put our names on each of these labels for our own families' catch. Karen's is on whatever Jessie and Pauli bring in. Mine's on my Jacks's. We work here because the state board of health says we got to, stainless steel tables and all, because we're processing food for resale and we can't no longer do it in our own out buildings or kitchens.

"Maybe we should learn that material things ought not define our success as women and men."

Leonard Pitts Jr.

So with a lot of people's help and God's grace, we opened this place so we could stay in business. And it's working out pretty well, I think. I wasn't sure we could all get along, 'specially since we're all used to working at home."

Karen added, "I kind of like the company here. Beats listening to the TV all day, just for some voices to hear. And together like this, it feels kind of, girly, you know? I mean, as if wearing jeans and occasionally working on the boats suddenly makes me a man and not a woman. I'm still a woman. But, not being so isolated and being around other women almost makes me feel I am in some girly job, like being a secretary or something and wearing pantyhose." She looked at Kelly. "You don't know what I'm talking about, do you?"

"I think so."

"Yeah, you probably do. Yes. Good for you, Kelly."

"Does Uncle Jesse work far out in the Bay?"

"Yes, he does. He's a crab potter and that takes him out deep on the Bay, not scraping along the shoals or trot-lining in the creeks. Bigger style of boat. Different kind of rhythm to the work."

"What kind of workday do you have here?"

"Early."

Joyce took over the lesson. "Our day starts when theirs does, around three in the morning. We have a little prayer, read from the Bible, sing some songs together and pick from the previous day's harvest. Then we pack up the containers of crab meat in ice and ship it on the ferry to the mainland before it leaves around seven in the morning. Some have their specific customers — restaurants, and they buy direct. Some go through a middleman. Pretty much everyone's got their own dependable source of delivery and payment. But we all do it here together."

"Does Pauli like it?"

"You'll have to ask her that one," Karen replied, somewhat diplomatically. "But I think she does. She will complain to anyone who will listen about spending her days pulling pots and culling crabs. And about how she used to get sick as a dog when she first started working with her dad. But last fall, during a long weekend from school, she went out with Jesse and caught herself a seagull." She began to laugh at the memory, and Joyce and Kelly began laughing along with her. "It seems a gull landed alongside of her, and she reached around and grabbed its leg. Startled the heck out of both of them. Jesse about busted a gut laughing so hard, and after about ten seconds or so, Pauli let that bird go, and it tore out of there."

The three women laughed at the image of a startled gull and equally startled Pauli. After a few seconds the laughter died down and the only sound for several moments was the rain lashing against the windows of the now darkened co-op. Joyce rose and turned on the light.

Kelly was curious. "You said you read from the Bible. You do that everyday? Why? Are you religious?"

Joyce answered first. "I guess all of us are, in some way. You see we don't have a mayor or a town council here on the island. The church is the main governing body. We got no elected officials here. And it works because it's small enough. There is also the spiritual side of working so close to nature. Most of us here see the Bay, and what she provides us, as a gift that we appreciate."

Karen added, "I think you'll find a strong sense of community here. Jesse and me feel free out here, not isolated like I sometimes think you and my sister must feel on the mainland. I'll give you an example. Everyone on the island goes to the school pageants, whether they have kids in school or not. And where else can you give the ferry boat captain your grocery list and a blank check and have your groceries delivered right to your door step? Now that is a convenience. There is a sense of belonging, of being part of something outside yourself. That is very special, and we don't ever want to lose it."

"Besides," Joyce continued, "Jesus hung around fishermen, commercial fishermen, up in

Galilee, so we kind of think that God is looking out for us, you know. So we begin each day with a little Bible read, though probably a bunch of us pray that the Bay will come back. Because we're just holding on, trying to keep our livelihood, and our freedom. That's why this co-op was born. We think we've got a good product and a good way of life, and this co-op will help keep this community together. Now," she finished with a twinkle in her eye, "I'll bet you didn't see me step up on my soapbox, did ya?"

Just then Spaghetti loped through the doorway and informed them that some of the boats' lights were spotted heading for the dock. Karen and Joyce both heaved a sigh and affectionately closed up the co-op. They headed for their respective homes knowing that their families would be in need of some hot coffee and soup.

Kelly sat out on the screened-in porch of Karen and Jesse's single-story house and waited. She quietly watched several golf carts and a few men pulling wheelbarrows from the docking area, but there was no sign of Jesse and Pauli. The rain continued, not as heavy as when it started, but still continuously, and fog soon engulfed the island. An hour later, a wheelbarrow was pulled into the yard and a lean, balding, bewhiskered Jesse and his stocky, tall daughter grabbed their gear from it and crossed onto the porch.

Karen greeted them first, with hugs and kisses. Jesse apologized for being late but reported that Lonny's boat slipped a shaft and needed a

tow, so they helped out and got him, slowly, back home, to the dock. Jesse and Pauli both seemed genuinely pleased to see Kelly. At the dinner table, Jesse asked Kelly to flex her right arm muscle, then complimented her on decking the teacher's aide, telling her he'd have done the same thing.

"Suspended!" He snorted. "No adult has a right to talk to a child like that. There may have been a better response on your part, Kelly, but I'd have given you a medal." He grinned, then turned to his daughter and asked with mock seriousness,

"Do you think Kelly is strong enough to work on the Bay?"

Karen replied for her. "If she's as strong than that, we could use her at the co-op."

"Ah," Jesse responded, "That takes real strength. I don't know a woman that doesn't work harder than any man on this island. What do you say, Kelly?"

Kelly grinned. "I think I'd like to try both, maybe."

"Good," Pauli enthused. "Now maybe

I can get a day without listening to my dad's horrible jokes."

With that remark, Uncle Jesse clasped his heart and pitched himself off his chair and onto the floor, moaning that no one loves him anymore, as wife and daughter groaned and laughed.

After supper, Kelly helped clean up the table and the dishes, and watched the family, knowing that each felt they belonged in the space. Suddenly she knew what connected them, what being a part of something felt like. She remembered the fear and the sharing of it without words. In the space of a day, she felt touched by the Bay, even though she could not utter a specific word or feeling for it. It just was.

The rain finally stopped, and the wind had died down and she sat on the porch in the dark of the night and listened to the sounds of the marsh. Somewhere in the distance, far back behind her in another room she heard someone singing:

"Leaning, leaning, safe and secure from all alarms. Leaning, leaning, leaning in HIS everlasting arms."

"Rack of eye'

means using your own
judgement and explains
the informal nature of
workboat building on
Smith Island. Boats are
built not to drafted
plans but according to a
design that existed in
the mind's eye."

Paula Johnson

Somerset County

Tylerton

"Where everyone needs a boat."

"That soft crab, he's the one you get paid for."

"There's no quick fix that will restore the Chesapeake or its grasses.
You just can't pass a bill that's going to bring it all back."

Larry Simns

Island of High Achievers

"Smith Island's crab pickers legalized with founding of co-op"
Article by A. Tyler Settle

A fight to the death has come to an end. Had the outcome of this four-year battle been different, the income vital to a good number of Smith Island's already strapped families would have been victimized. Dead would have been a generation's old custom.

But, conquering the odds stacked against them, some Smith Island women have come out on top.

Led to victory by Janis Marshall of Tylerton, 14 crab pickers have preserved not only their necessary income, but also a time honored tradition on the tiny Chesapeake Bay island. The fateful mission was accomplished with the late June founding of the Smith Island Crab Co-op. Now these ladies are picking and grinning. And, they're legal.

For nearly as long as watermen and their families have made Smith Island their home, women have picked crabs in out-kitchens adjoining their houses. Through solitary work, this home picking was profitable and allowed the women, most of them wives and mothers, to tend to the needs of their families while eking out a living. Satisfying their customers on the mainland, the crab pickers also fortified their families' earnings.

All was well until the state's Health Department began to eye these home businesses as suspect. In question were not the final goods, which met all the health requirements, but the methods used to produce them. While most pickers used stainless steel knives and pans, some lacked stainless steel scales, tables or other equipment. The Health Department began to furrow its regulatory brow.

The suspicion climaxed on the dock in Crisfield one pivotal day in 1992, when Natural Resource Police and a health inspector confiscated 35 pounds of crabmeat Mrs. Marshall had picked and was bringing to the mainland.

Apparently, the Health Department had decided to crack down and force Smith Island to adhere to the standards applied to the rest of the

Bay. Though Mrs. Marshall wonders if health officials targeted or chose to use Smith Island crab pickers as an example for any questionable crab picker throughout the bay because "we're all in a concentrated area and easy to catch," she's not one to hold a grudge. In fact, she and her sister co-op members are thrilled with the feat of establishing and now running a business. At the same time, they are able to uphold the tradition of crab picking, which they inherited from their foremothers.

Operating a co-op business is new to these women and they have developed a sophisticated system to make it work. "None of us had any business background and we've worked out a system by trial and error," Mrs. Marshall said, emphasizing the democracy that rules the co-op, the undertone of which is unintentionally feminist.

Each woman picks her own crabs, which are brought in by the watermen and tagged with the woman's name before being put into the steamer. After the picking is done, the meat goes into specially designed containers, which are put into boxes, each distinguished by a woman's name penned on the side. When an order comes in, whichever woman has claim to that customer completes her paper work and transports the crabmeat via hand cart down to the county dock.

Of each picker's profit, $2 per pound goes back into the co-op. Should a large order be placed, the women's stocks are rotated, so that each gets a crack at it.

The chores are evenly divided and each week a different woman takes the helm and sees to the bookkeeping and other operational tasks. Lest there be any confusion about whose turn it is, a board in the building's foyer reads, "Any questions or complaints, see Tina," who was taking her turn recently.

With the evolution of the co-op has come not only peace of mind as far as the Health Department is concerned but also a sense of accomplishment.

As she proudly paraded visitors around the co-op recently, Mrs. Marshall beamed even more brightly as she gingerly removed from its place of honor on the wall, the Health Department-issued license.

She said, "This is our prized possession. We've had a frame for this for over a month and we finally got the license in the mail yesterday. It took four years to get this piece of paper — like a college degree." A bonus is the social opportunities allowed now that these women are working outside their homes. "We've been raised on this island and we all know each other, go to church together but this has given us a chance to come out of our houses and go to work together."

Indeed, the pickers gather around the

huge stainless steel table to pick their crabs and the chatter is incessant. The group jokes, talks a bit of politics, reads from the Bible, and even sings hymns and other songs, the lyrics for which they come up with themselves.

"It's like a family with lots of kids, and when a family gets together, a lot goes on," Mrs. Marshall explained. "Somebody will pass an opinion every once in awhile, and that's ok, too."

This, then, is a family of high achievers. It took guts with no sights set on glory to get the ball rolling toward legalizing their way of life and Janis Marshall was the momentum. After her crabmeat was confiscated by state health inspectors, an incensed Mrs. Marshall sought the help of Senator Lowell Stolfzus. She said she approached him with the idea he would help her bypass the system. Instead, he advised her how to go about legitimizing the business of picking crabs. Innumerable grant proposals, contracts, hits and misses later, Mrs. Marshall secured the money to make it happen.

The state provided $83,000 and the Farmers Home Administration, $115,000. A $15,000 loan from the University of Maryland's Rural Development Center came through, as did loans from Dewey Beach Enterprises and Franklin P. Perdue, both to the tune of $10,000.

Though the crab season's sluggish

kickoff was hurting the co-op initially, as were the island's remaining pirate pickers, Mrs. Marshall expects the fortune that has graced her group thus far to continue.

And longtime fans of the pickers' crabmeat hope so too.

Jay Perttyman, proprietor of the Rusty Rudder, Crabbers' Cove and the Lighthouse Restaurant, all in Dewey Beach, Delaware, says he bought from the ladies before they were legal. When they were shut down, Perttyman was sorely disappointed to lose a product so vital to his menus. "These are nice people, and they just want to make a living," Perttyman said. "Me, I'd rather have their crabmeat than anybody else's."

-ATS

BAKED IMPERIAL ROCKFISH

Recipe by Janice Marshall

1 large Rockfish	5 strips of bacon	fı stick margarine
1 pound crabmeat	4 tablespoons flour	2 tablespoons mayonnaise
2 pounds potatoes	fı cup evaporated milk	1 teaspoon mustard
1 large onion	fı cup water	Old Bay seasoning to taste

Clean and wash fish. Salt and pepper to taste. Lay bacon strips on rack of baking pan. Place fish on rack on top of bacon strips. Set aside. In frying pan melt margarine, 2 tablespoons flour and stir. Add milk and water mixture. Stir until thick paste. Remove from heat. Add mayonnaise, mustard and Old Bay to taste. Mix in crabmeat. Stuff fish with mixture. Put bacon around fish and secure with tooth picks. Spray sheet cake pan with Pam. Sprinkle 2 tablespoons flour on bottom of pan. Peel and slice potatoes. Put fish on rack in sheet pan. Spread potatoes in bottom of pan. Peel and slice onion over fish and potatoes. Pour 1 1/2 cups water over all. Cover with foil and bake 350 degrees about 1 1/2 hours. Remove foil and bake until bacon and fish are brown. No more than 15 minutes. Remove from oven and let set for 10 minutes. Serve on platter with potato and gravy. Serve with applesauce and cornbread.

PATIENCE AND A LITTLE HELP FROM MOTHER NATURE

"Waterman's wife grows to appreciate new lifestyle"
Letter to the Editor

Though born and raised on the Chesapeake Bay, the Waterman was a person I was not familiar with. He seemed to be just a guy on a boat who rode past our house in the early morning. Of course I was always asleep so I never got a glimpse of him. Four doors down lived our neighbor Mac McNasby, who owned McNasbys Oyster Company in Annapolis. Little did I know my future would cruise in that direction. When I met my husband Kenny he was not working on the water, although he had in the past. We fell in love and got married to live happily ever after. Soon after we were married, Kenny came home from work — he was working for my dad — and announced he was going back to his real love: working as a Waterman. I looked at him and thought to myself, "You've got to be kidding!" He wasn't. He borrowed some money to buy his first boat.

In all his excitement, the day finally came when he took me to see his new vessel. I took one look and scratched my head, thinking that there was no way it would ever stay afloat. But lo and behold, he fixed the boat up, repaired the engine, and added a roof so the crabs wouldn't bake in the sun.

Meanwhile, our front lawn had turned into a crab pot assembly line. What had once been my view of green grass and flowers was now galvanized wire, zincs, floats, cord and cull rings. Ken worked for hours creating crab pots, and I would watch and wonder how this was possibly going to work out.

The time came to set the pots, so Ken bought the bait and let the pots sit for a couple of days, which meant he was home again. By this time I was eager for him to go to work, but at least I could see my front yard again since the crab pots were gone.

Then the bad news. A red tide came in and killed the bait. Ever the optimist, Ken said, "No problem! I'll just move the pots and rebait." Needless to say, I was feeling a little shaky about this whole Waterman career thing. Finally, the first good day of crabbing came and I thought, "Hallelujah! Maybe, just maybe, this will work!"

Now after ten years of marriage, my education of the Waterman's way of life has blossomed. What I thought would never get off the ground has proven me wrong. Hard work, long hours, patience and a little help from Mother Nature has made this a special way of life.

My husband goes to work in a good mood and comes home in a good mood — what else could I ask for?

Karen Keen

BEAUTY IS WHERE YOU LOOK

"Oysterman awed by the natural beauty of his catch"
Article by A. Tyler Settle

It's nearly impossible to tell that Kenny Keen has been working the water for much of his life. This Dunkirk-based waterman is so awed by the high quality of the oysters he drops from the tongs to the culling board, it's easy to believe he just started as a commercial harvester. "This is all natural," he yells over the bellow of the patent tongs, waving overhead an impressive clump of oysters plucked from the waters off Solomon's Island. "Never been planted. Beautiful. Just beautiful," Keen exclaims at another point, putting the oyster's huge shell to his lips for an appreciative kiss.

CALVERT COUNTY

Solomons

Keen's enthusiasm for his catch is refreshing on a good day and inspiring on a day like the one in early February, when the precipitation ranged from sleet to snow to relentless rain.

His unbridled admiration for those oysters is matched only by his skill at locating and harvesting them. Keen's sure hands and steady feet mocked the howling weather and sleet-slicked deck. As he worked the patent tongs with such ease, and even grace, his task looked deceptively simple. There is no mistaking the amount of time this man has spent on the water, honing and now having mastered his trade. Tongful after tongful of oysters came aboard the double rigged **LONG SHOT** under Keen's able hand.

And these oysters were, indeed, exquisite. Just as their crustacean counterparts, the crabs, have been dubbed "beautiful swimmers," these treasures could be called the same — similar in their beauty, that is. These jewels, of course, stay stationary to be scooped up by those like Keen, who are so deeply devoted to the lifestyle that they go after the bivalves even on days of such inclement weather that many folks choose to stay indoors, far from the frigid, windy waters of the bay.

But Keen and others continue their pursuit of this way of making a living, even in the face of disease and other menaces threatening the oyster population. Some good news recently, though. The oyster harvest as of February was 1,116,673 bushels and the value was $2.3 million, according to preliminary figures from the Department of Natural Resources. The price per bushel was running between $18 and $22 and some of the prime harvest areas were in waterways marred in years past by disease.

The 1997 "spat set" broke records but in doing so presented some confusion early this season. So many spat (baby oysters) were attached to market-sized oysters that watermen were in a quandary as to what to do: leave the market oyster in the name of saving the spat for future harvesting or take the market and prevent the spat's chance at growing into harvestable crop later? Some natural resource officers were also confused and misinterpreted the law to say any market oyster with spat must go into the 5 percent cup.

As it turns out, the law had not changed but needed a bit of clarification. The law reads that any oyster less than three inches, whether attached to a market oyster or not, must be included in the culling and replaced on the bar from which it was caught.

However, "the Department by rule may permit the possession of marketable oyster to which nonmarketable oysters adhere so closely that it is impossible to remove them without destroying the smaller oyster. A person may possess marketable oysters or spat less than one inch in length from hinge to bill attached to them that cannot be separated without destroying the small oyster," according to the Annotated Code of Maryland.

-ATS

Fish are like Birds

"Week long closure of gill net fishery prompted by plethora of fish"

Article by A.Tyler Settle

The day before the commercial striped bass gill-net fishery was prematurely shut down, Bob Evans' nets were teeming with fish. It was not striped bass, though, that filled the Churchton waterman's nets. It was perch. On the afternoon of Feb. 6, Evans' boat **TEMPEST** docked with only 300 pounds of striped bass — half his daily quota. The deck was overtaken instead by perch still clinging to the net's mesh.

Even though the perch would fetch but 50 cents a pound, it was a profitable catch, for the price of striped bass had dropped a dollar per pound in just three days, due to the recently near-extinct fish's overabundance. Fishermen from the Virginia-Maryland line, and all the way up the bay were catching their quota and catching it fast. That flood of fish is what prompted the week-long closure. Too many watermen were catching their limit so quickly that the projected quota it was feared, would be exceeded. The fishery was scheduled to continue through Feb. 28, or until the 1,325,680 pound quota was harvested.

Just a day before the fishery was to reopen, the Department of Natural Resources announced the reduction in daily quota from 200 pounds to 150 pounds. DNR officials said the daily limit must be reduced to allow the completion of the February season. Also, the tributary fishermen and those in the Crisfield area had to be assured they would be left some fish to catch. In the meantime, Evans said he was one of the lucky ones because his boat is rigged to fish for either striped bass or perch.

Another waterman, Leo James, said he too had targeted the plentiful perch but abandoned the plan when the price dipped to 30 cents per pound. Before then, however, James said he had pulled in more than 5 tons, which made the 40-50 cents per pound price tag worth pursuing. "There was a fish in every mesh," James said.

"Up until two days ago, we were catching our limit everyday," according to Evans, who said the previous week found his boat weighing in with tons of fish. However, the next couple of days he ended up with 300 pounds and than 150 pounds of rockfish. That's when he turned to perch.

Evans was in full support of the closure. In fact, he endorses the system he dubs 'state of the art'. "We can shut it down and tally up how much we have left in our seasonal quota; it's a good system that works."

Still, fish will be fish. And fish are unpredictable. "They move all the time, they are like birds that way."

-ATS

Epilogue

By Steve Burch

Henry David Thoreau once wrote that the majority of us lead lives of quiet desperation. Bound by our jobs, our responsibilities to ourselves and our families, life frequently feels jagged and jarring, nonstop and without succor. Our frantic pursuit of material gain and our consumerism have obscured the needs of our souls and our spirituality is drowned out by the desires of the moment.

Herman Melville opens **MOBY DICK** by observing the inhabitants of a port city drawn as if by a mysterious force down to the sea: **What do you see?— Posted like silent sentinels all around the town, stand thousands upon thousands of mortal men fixed in ocean reveries. Some leaning against the spiles; some seated upon pierheads; some looking over the bulkwards of ships from China; some high aloft in the rigging, as if the striving to get a still better seaward peep. But these are all landsmen; of week days pent up in lath and plaster — tied to counters, nailed to benches,** clinched to desks. How then this? Are the fields gone? What do   they hear?

I suspect it is not merely some childhood daydream of piracy, but rather a yearning for a life that still rewards the soul. The people who continue to work the water — on their boats, on their land — stay in a changing, sometimes inhospitable climate because something deep within each and every one of them is fed by their work on the Bay. Whether one is pulling up the traps or packaging the oysters or clams in a land based co-op, there is little if any romance to be lived in this hardscrabble life. Yet these people stay. True, in ever-diminishing numbers. But many continue the work of their parents and grandparents and great-grandparents, through disastrous storms, industrial pollution, cultural indifference, bureaucratic overregulation, and disappointing harvest. And their lives are all the richer for it.

NOTE TO COLLECTORS OF BLACK AND WHITE PRINTS

A sales pitch

You can hang on your wall an original 5 x 7 inch black and white photographic print matted and signed by the photographer.

Just send a note and the title and page number of the print you want along with a check for $45.00 to James Parker for the purchase price plus the state sales tax of 5% and $5.00 for shipping. To: P/O Box 1353, Severna Park, Maryland 21146-1353.

"Of all the means of expression, photography is the only one that fixes a precise moment in time."

Henri Cartier-Bresson

"The harder you work, the more you make and what you make is yours."

Calvin Goutgh

LIST OF
PHOTOGRAPHIC PRINTS

Pg. 3, CHANGING THE OYSTER DREDGE. 1984
On board the skipjack Kathryn under sail

Pg. 8-9, MANEUVERING FOR THE START. 1990
Chesapeake Appreciation Days skipjack races

Pg. 11, REBECCA T. RUARK. 1990
Oyster Dredge boat license # 29,
Wade Murphy, Captain

Pg. 12, NO WIND FOR A RACE. 1989
C. A. Days, Sandy Point State Park,
Anne Arundel Co.

Pg. 13, SKIPJACKS ON A BROAD REACH. 1991
Chesapeake Appreciation Days skipjacks races

Pg. 15, FREEWHEELING WATERMAN. 1992
Sandy Point Sate Park, Anne Arundel County

Pg. 16-17, SKIPJACKS ON PARADE. 1993
Sandy Point State Park, Anne Arundel County

Pg. 19, SKIPJACKS. 1993
Sandy Point State Park, Anne Arundel County

Pg. 21, HOISTING SAIL. 1989
Sandy Point State Park, Anne Arundel County

Pg. 22-23, SKIPJACKS AND SANDY POINT LIGHT.
1992
Sandy Point State Park, Anne Arundel County

Pg. 24, MINNIE V. 1983

Pg. 25, PUSHBOAT ON THE BEACH. 1991
Skipjack Sigsbee
Sandy Point State Park, Anne Arundel County

Pg. 26, SURVIVOR. 1997
Back River Neck, Baltimore County

Pg. 28, EDDIE FORD. 1982
Hart-Miller Island, Baltimore County

Pg. 29, EELS. 1982
Baltimore County

Pg. 30, REPAIRING A FYKE NET. 1996
Baltimore County

Pg. 31, FYKE NET. 1996
Bush River, Harford County

Pg. 32, OFF-LOADING CATFISH. 1996
Bush River, Harford County

Pg. 33, POUND NET. 1996
Susquehanna Flats, Cecil County

Pg. 34, DIP NET. 1996
Susquehanna Flats, Cecil County

Pg. 39, BOAT YARD. 1995
Rockhall, Kent County

Pg. 40, WATERMAN'S CRABHOUSE. 1982
Rockhall, Kent County

Pg. 41, BOAT SHEDS. 1995
Rockhall, Kent County

Pg. 42, GAS DOCK. 1982
Rockhall, Kent County

Pg. 43, STRIPED BASS. 1993
New Years Day, Dawn II, Rockhall

Pg. 45, WATERMAN. 1996
Rockhall, Kent County

Pg. 46-47, FISH FRY. 1996
Rockhall, Kent County

Pg. 48, OYSTER 'PATENT' TONG BOATS. 1982
Rockhall, Kent County

Pg. 49, OYSTERMAN WITH 'PATENT' TONG. 1982
Rockhall, Kent County

Pg. 50, HYDRAULIC SOFT SHELL CLAM DREDGE.
1996
Clam Boat 'Emma-Sara', Rockhall

Pg. 51, THOMAS 'MAGNUM' LUKENICH. 1996
Clam Boat 'Emma-Sara', Rockhall

Pg. 52, 'BEAR'. 1982
Clam Boat 'Dawn', Rockhall

Pg. 53, CLAM BOAT. 1982
'Dawn', Rockhall

Pg. 54, OYSTERMAN. 1984
Piney Point, Choptank River

Pg. 55, OYSTER 'SHAFT' TONGS. 1984
Grasonville, Queen Annes County

Pg. 56, CRAB SHANTY. 1983
Kent Narrows, Queen Annes County

Pg. 57, CRAB POTS. 1990
Bloody Point, Queen Annes County

Pg. 58-59, SKIPJACK 'ELSWORTH'. 1983
Tilghman Island, Talbot County

Pg. 60, SKIPJACK 'ELSWORTH'. 1984
Tilghman Island, Talbot County

Pg. 61, CAPTAIN RUSSELL DIZE. 1986
Skipjack 'Kathryn', Harris Creek

Pg. 62-63, FURLING THE MAIN SAIL. 1986
Skipjack "Kathryn", Choptank River

Pg. 64, OYSTER 'CULLING'. 1985
'Kathryn', Choptank River

Pg. 65, WILL FIXES SPAGHETTI. 1985
Skipjack 'Elsworth', Tilghman Island

Pg. 62-63, GOING HOME. 1986
Skipjack 'Kathryn', Tilghman Island

Pg. 68, TILGHMAN ISLAND BRIDGE. 1986
Tilghman Island, Talbot County

Pg. 69, CHARTER BOAT 'ANNE ARUNDEL'. 1993
Knapps Narrows, Tilghman Island

Pg. 70-71, CRAB POTS. 1994
Brenda II, Tilghman Island

Pg. 72, FRONT PORCH. 1987
Tilghman Island, Talbot County

Pg. 73, GRACE E. II.1987
Tilghman Island, Talbot County

Pg. 74, SKIPJACK 'LORRANIE ROSE'. 1984
Knapps Narrows, Talbot County

Pg. 75, BASKET SITTER. 1987
Tilghman Island, Talbot County

Pg. 76, HOUSE. 1984
Richland Point, Dorchester County

Pg. 77, SKIPJACK MODEL. 1986
Hoopers Island, Dorchester County

Pg. 78, FEMALE 'SHOOK' BLUE CRAB. 1988
Hoopers Island, Dorchester County

Pg. 79, WIND, WAVES & CLOUDS. 1990
Fishing Creek, Dorchester County

Pg. 81, CRAB BOAT. 1995
Toddville, Dorchester County

Pg. 82, CRAB BOAT WITH TREES. 1995
Toddville, Dorchester County

Pg. 84, MAIN STREET. 1998
Elliot Island, Dorchester County

Pg. 88, METHODIST CHURCH. 1998
St. Stephens, Somerset County

Pg. 89, DECEMBER 25TH. 1998
St. Stephens, Somerset County

Pg. 91, CRAB POTS. 1998
Deal Island, Somerset County

Pg. 92-93, UPPER THOROUGHFARE. 1998
Chance, Somerset County

Pg. 94, BASKETS OF FISH. 1998
Bivalve, Somerset County

Pg. 95, FRED MADDOX. 1998
Pocomoke River, Somerset County

Pg. 96, MISS NORMA. 1982
Tyler Creek, Somerset County

Pg. 97, SMITH ISLAND. 1982
Tylerton, Somerset County

Pg. 98, 'DANA-CHRISTINE'. 1982
Tylerton, Somerset County

Pg. 99, WAVERLY EVANS. 1996
Tylerton, Somerset County

Pg. 100-101, BOY IN A BOAT. 1982
Tyler Creek, Somerset County

Pg. 102, CRAB MEAT PICKED BY PATTY. 1996
Tylerton, Somerset County

Pg. 104, SHORELINE. 1996
Tylerton, Somerset County

Pg. 105, STRIPED 'ROCKFISH' BASS. 1996
Chesapeake Bay

Pg. 107, 'LONG SHOT'. 1996
Solomans, Calvert County

Pg. 108, KENNY KEEN. 1996
Hog Point, Calvert County

Pg. 109, OYSTER ON THE HALF SHELL. 1990
Chesapeake Bay

Pg. 110, BOB EVANS. 1996
Shady Side, Anne Arundel County

Pg. 112, 'CAPT'N BUNKY'. 1995
Shady Side, Anne Arundel County

Pg. 113, MCNASBY'S SEAFOOD. 1993
Back Creek, Anne Arundel County

Pg. 114, ANNAPOLIS HARBOR. 1995
Back Creek, Anne Arundel County

Pg. 119, 'PATENT' TONG OYSTER RIGS. 1985
Annapolis, Anne Arundel County

THE END

Brief Descriptions of Commercial Seafood and Harvesting Styles

The important commercial seafoods harvested from the Chesapeake Bay include blue crab (hard crabs, soft crabs, and crab meat), striped bass (rockfish), oysters, soft clams, eels and catfish.

The **ATLANTIC BLUE CRAB, Calli-nectes sapidus,** are proficient swimmers owing to their fifth pair of legs, or paddles. The muscle associated with these paddles are the succulent morsels of seafood known as lump meat or back-fin. The commercial industry that harvests this pugnacious and aggressive animal developed in the mid-19th century with the advent of refrigeration through manufactured ice. Crabs are very predatory and will eat just about anything they can successfully attack. There are three basic ways to harvest the hard shelled Atlantic blue crab.

1. **CRAB POTS** are baited wire cubes left in the water to trap crabs 24 hours a day. Designed by Benjamin F. Lewis in 1938, they were outlawed in 1941 for being too efficient, which seems to be a recurring problem. Legalized again in 1943, they are now restricted to the deeper waters of the Chesapeake Bay proper. For photographs of Crab Pots see pages 42, 57 and 70,

2. The oldest method of harvesting blue crabs is the **TROTLINE**. Baited with salted eel, bull lips, or chicken necks, it is a strong cotton or nylon rope in excess of 1000 feet. It is not as costly as potting, nor is it as efficient. It is usually set before dawn in the calm waters of the Chesapeake's tributaries and needs to be actively fished.

3. In the shallows of the lower Eastern Shore some watermen use the **CRAB SCRAPE.**

Crab Trotline

Patented by L. Cooper Dize of Crisfield, Maryland in 1870, it is a light-weight, toothless dredge similar in nature to the oyster dredge. It works like scraping the crumbs off the dinner table into a bag. Because the dredge has no teeth, it is not very harmful.

THE STRIPED BASS, Morone saxatilis

Crab Scrape

(dumb as a rock), known locally as 'rockfish' and 'stripers', are semi-anadromous fish that must seek fresh water to reproduce. They are adventurous fish leaving the bay in the late winter for the Atlantic ocean, migrating as far north as Nova Scotia. Striped bass are commercially harvested with two styles of nets according to their natural movement and the limits of the law.

1. Introduced in Maryland in 1858, the **POUND NET** is a stationary trap formed of nets supported on stakes. Although historically important, it is no longer in widespread use because it is costly to purchase and maintain. Today it reflects a bait-food chain operation, providing bait fish for the crabbing industry along with food for the table when fishing regulations permit.

For photographs of Pound Nets, see pages 33 and 34.

2. The **DRIFT NET** is a barrier of gill netting set across the predicted path of schooling fish. It is a selective harvesting technique where smaller fish can swim through the net. Location, seasonal use, hours of operation, and net size are highly regulated by the government in its effort to manage fish populations. Recreational fishing interests hold this technique responsible for a high mortality rate. Yet in 1995, Massachusetts found that 262,000 stripers died after release by sport anglers, compared to a total commercial harvest of 41,000 fish.

For photographs of Drift Net fishing, see page 43.

The **CHESAPEAKE OYSTER, Crassostrea virginica**, is a filter feeding bivalve mollusk without beauty, grace, or charm. Its ability to survive extended periods of time out of the water (in cool weather) helped fuel the western migration of this country. It is high in iron, and rumor has it, good for the sex life. The tradition of eating oysters during the months whose names contain an **r** is biologically based on the lack of flavor and quality during and after they spawn in the early summer. The oyster is responsible for the first conservation laws. There are three basic styles used in harvesting oysters today and they are nearly identical to those used a century ago.

1. The most widely used method of gathering oysters is the **SHAFT** or **HAND TONG**, which are rake-like wire baskets attached to two long sticks fastened together like scissors. The ideal stick is 12 to 30 feet long and made from the heartwood of long leaf Georgia pine. Shaft tonging is physically demanding, requiring strength, balance, and dexterity. It is the Waterman with the biggest shirt who hand tongs for oysters. The investment in gear is modest, and the shaft tonger usually works in the shallow rivers and creeks, which are off-limits to oystermen using other types of gear.

For photographs of Shaft Tonging, see pages 54 and 55.

Shaft or Hand Tongs

2. **PATENT TONGS** are used to reach the oyster bars in the deep waters of the Chesapeake Bay proper. Originally the tongs were dropped to the bottom and hand winched back to the boat. In 1958, hydraulic power enhanced the speed of the rig, starting the evolution of resource use and decline. It is expensive, efficient, and operated by foot pedals and levers that makes patting your head and rubbing your stomach at the same time seem easy.

For Patent Tong photographs, see pages 48-49, 108, 113-114 and 118.

3. The oyster-gathering tool we love to hate is the **OYSTER DREDGE**. Introduced to Maryland in 1808, prohibited in 1820, reinstated in 1865, responsible for the oyster wars of the 1860's, 70's and 80's, the oyster dredge is so efficient it can only be used by sailboats. It is a simple triangular metal frame with a toothed raking bar no wider than 44 inches, to which is attached a bag. Lowered to the bottom with a steel cable, the oyster dredge is dragged behind the boat, collecting everything in its path.

After each 'lick' on the bottom, the dredge, full of mud, old shell and oysters, is power winched to the surface. The crew manfully dumps the debris on the deck, then bends over to 'cull' for the live oysters of three inches or larger.

If you were part of that crew your day would start at 3 a.m., and you would be wet and cold, and your knees would hurt before most people have read the morning sports page. The wind blows up your butt as your pile of 'keeper' oysters grows. A little warmth is available during lunch, then it's back to work. At a state-regulated hour, you stop. Wash down begins and the race to be the first one home is at hand. While maintenance chores are done, the warm yellow winter light turns the Bay a deep blue, and the wind sings a homeward song into the sails. It is exciting to beat the other boats to the dock and your worth as a member of the crew will soon be measured in tallied bushels of oysters. Crisp twenty dollar bills dance in your head as you calculate your percentage . The world is good, the Bay has been kind, and the captain smart. Then onto the boat steps 'the law', with black shiny shoes, razor creased green pants, and a gun.

For more photographs of Oyster Dredging, see pages 58-67.

The **SOFT-SHELL CLAM, Mya arenaria,** is a burrowing bivalve harvested from the mid-bay region. Local appreciation is not widespread and most are now sent north to satisfy New Englanders' taste for 'steamers'.

The most efficient method of harvesting the clams without breaking their brittle shells is the **HYDRAULIC CLAM DREDGE,** developed by Fletcher Hank. High-pressured water is used to liquefy the bottom and mine out the clams. The delicate clams are then carried upwards on a chain-meshed conveyor to the side of the boat. There are a number of controversies surrounding the clamming industry. During the striped bass moratorium many watermen turned to clamming depressing the market and placing a strain on the species. Then there was a handling and shipping problem which was resolved with proper refrigeration. And now, there is a concern about dredge damage done to the Bays' remaining beds of sea grass. The Waterman community is aware of the importance of good environmental stewardship. The future of their industry hinges on proper management and Bay restoration. There is no advantage in habitat destruction for short term gain.

For photographs of Clams, see pages 50-53.

"I am the master of my fate:
I am the captain of my soul."

William Ernest Henley

EELS, Anquilla rostrata are snake-like, slimy fish exported to Europe via air freight. Eels are good tasting white fish, if you can get past the way they look and feel. Don't ever turn up the opportunity to try some barbecued. The most popular method of catching eels is with a baited trap or 'pot'. Most pots are round cylinders with the openings facing into the tide. I have been told that you can't catch an eel in the southern part of the bay in a round pot; they have to be square. Razor clams and horseshoe crabs are the bait of choice. There are some controversies over the collecting of horseshoe crabs to be used as bait. Migrating shore birds feed off the eggs of the crabs and there are fears that over-harvesting will affect bird populations.

For photographs of Eels, see pages 28 and 29.

CATFISH, Ameiurus nebulosus, Ameiurus catus, or Ictalurus punctatus, are smooth-skinned fish lacking scales, with long cat-like whiskers. The male fish usually guard and herd the offspring until they are about fi inch long. Most catfish are trapped in a shallow water cylindrical net supported by 3 to 6 hoops called **FYKE NETS.** The nets are generally 10 feet long and 48 inches in diameter, with a leader and wings bringing the fish to a funneled opening. Most catfish trapped in the upper bay during the spring are shipped live to the South.

For photographs of Fyke Nets , see pages 30 and 31.

The most essential tool of the Chesapeake working waterman is the **DEADRISE WORK BOAT**. With many exceptions, it is basically a motorized craft of 20 to 30 feet in length made of wood or fiberglass. The boats constructed of wood are framed with cross planking, or long planked. The bottoms are round, flat, or v-shaped, and their width (beam) is usually one third of their length. The design or layout of the crafts is a reflection of the individual waterman's ideas about how a boat should be. Many of the boats are home built without plans. Almost all of the boats are referred to as 'she', for they bear the responsibility of life and are working partners.

The last boats working under sail in the United States are the oyster dredge boats commonly known as **SKIPJACKS**. They are wide, flat-decked working platforms, powered by wind, that fulfill the amended conservation law of 1865. No one seems to know where the term Skipjack comes from or how it identifies a style of boat, except that any oyster dredge boat with more than one mast is called a 'two-sail' or 'three-sail' bateaux. There is also the 'bugeye-rigged' bateaux which has a hull more narrow in proportion to length. It would be safe to say that a skipjack is a flat-bottomed, deadrise, box-built, jib-headed sloop wide of beam with hard chines that dredges for oysters.

"Being on a boat all your life — that boat becomes part of you"

Capt. Ruby G. Forf

Selected References

The following works have been of particular value

Life in the Chesapeake Bay
Alice Jane Lippson & Robert L. Lippson
1984, 1997, Johns Hopkins University Press

Working the Water
Edited By Paula J. Johnson
1988, University of Virginia Press
Calvert Marine Museum

Watermen of the Chesapeake
Mick Blackistone
1988, Acropolis Books

Rivers of the Eastern Shore
Hulbert Footner
1944, Farrar & Rienhart

The Workboats of Smith Island
Paula J. Johnson
1997, Johns Hopkins University Press

The Oysterback Tales
Hellen Chapple
1994, Johns Hopkins University Press

Run to the Lee
Kenneth F. Brooks, Jr.
1965, Johns Hopkins University Press

Pirates on the Chesapeake
Donald G. Shomette
1985, Tidewater Publishers

Notes on Chesapeake Bay Skipjacks
Howard I. Chapple
Chesapeake Bay Maritime Museum

The Last Waterman
Glenn Lawson
1988, Crisfield Publishing Company

American Dreams
Studs Turkel
1980, Pantheon Books

A Promise of Love
Alice Butler Bradshaw
1996, Brentwood Christian Press

Crab's Hole
Anne Hughes Jander
1994, Literary House Press

Nothing in this Book is Properly Documented

My apologies to Elaine Eff and every historian and academic in my life. You gave me every tool needed to do it correctly and well, you know, I was lucky to graduate. So even without the proper indexing or footnotes, efforts have been made to identify and acknowledge everyone. If you can hear yourself in any of the fictional characters, it is more than likely you who said it.

I traded a lot of tee-shirts for stories at the Waterman's Convention for a lot of years and I have a lot of tape, both audio and video. I even wrote some things down, quotes that were printed in the newspaper or maybe from a book. I don't remember where most of it came from. It might have something to do with growing up in the sixties, but the lack of brain cells is no excuse. I do need to thank Walter (Capt. Irving) and Bill Cummings for something that was special, but I can't remember what it was.

THE MORALITY OF SAVING THE BAY

Need drives all action

At times I wonder how to measure environmental success. I need to know that the water will be clean enough not to make me sick. I want reassurance that the economy will continue to provide me with toilet paper. And, I fear gentrification as much as toxic waste.

What I gain from a healthy bay has nothing to do with economics. The conflict between my current consumer choices and my emerging view of substantiality forces me to seek a balance that can only be found spiritually. It is important to support environmental restoration and the working communities of the Chesapeake Bay, for they define my 'sense of place' and provide me with a moral identity.

Social and environmental responsibility need to become a competitive advantage. By understanding the needs of my neighbors, and nature is one of them, I can gain a spiritual edge in decision making.

When the waters of the Chesapeake Bay become clean enough that no group of individuals could ever harvest all the food that she grows, then we will have environmental success. The vitality of the human occupations that have a distinctive connection to nature is of importance for what it adds to our understanding of how life works. There is a spiritual value of being around people who still make their living from a natural environment. The gift harvested from the Chesapeake Bay is best appreciated by those who depend on it to raise their families.

"Just as a fish doesn't understand water, I don't know that we fully understand what day-to-day life is like."

Kathleen Christensen

To order more books or send one to a friend or neighbor with a personal inscription contact **James Parker** at **P/O Box 1353, Severna Park, Maryland 21146** or call **410-647-3318**. Pay only $16.75 plus $3.20 for shipping when sending a book to a friend. Receive a 40% discount and free shipping for any order of twelve or more books. You can also order a matted print of any photograph in this book for $45.00.